a collection of recipes from the fam

the fresh market
& FRIENDS

First Edition

Layout and design by Insync Creative, Greensboro, NC

ISBN Number: 0-9723469-0-2

Library of Congress Card Number: 2002116354

FOREWORD

Dear Friends,

In 1982, my wife, Beverly and I opened a small store dedicated to providing quality foods in a friendly atmosphere. Over the past 20 years we have grown because of the dedication of our customers who enjoy the same high quality and amiable service we do. So it only seemed natural after all this time to create a cookbook celebrating this joy of food and friendship, and it could only happen if we included the favorite creations of our cherished customers.

I am very happy to share this collection of beloved recipes from your well used, dog-eared 3x5 index cards and time-honored family favorites. We appreciated your patience as we tested and contacted many of you to make sure we were doing your recipe justice in our kitchen. I hope you will all be as pleased with the results as I am. Our first collaborative effort is not an intimidating glossy book of technically impossible towers of food, but rather a realistic approach to everyday cooking. Some of our recipes are quite short, like our time! Other recipes are long and festive, recipes for celebratory times shared with treasured friends and loved ones. Overall this book is a delightful representation of the culinary talents within our growing circle of friends. I hope you will all enjoy this collection as much as we had in compiling it.

I would like to recognize the efforts of "The Fresh Market Cookbook Bunch" for their diligent work. I want to thank Susan Bohn for her culinary expertise, her stamina in "the heat of the kitchen" and her patience with those less skilled than she. To Diane Cleven, living proof that perpetual motion and endless energy are not relegated to physical theorists, thank you for your guidance, management, and great taste. This book is already a success because of your heart and dedication. To Melissa Boythe, our careful scrivener, thank you for your attention to detail and buoyant attitude as you deciphered and decoded the best-intentioned (though sometimes barely legible) submissions. Finally, to Heather Patton, thank you for your quiet, accurate, and persistent testing of recipes.

Most importantly I would like to thank all of you who shared your delicious recipes with us. We have done our best to acknowledge all of you on the following pages. We only wish we had room to print them all.

I thank you all for your continued support of great food and friendship, and I look forward to our next collaboration!

Ray Berry
Founder

CONTRIBUTORS

Eric and Gloria Adler
Julia Allen
Jennifer Andrews
Gloria Aumack
Suzanne Austin
Bill and Jane Bailey
Tucker Bailey
Mark Bairas
Mariana Magill Banasik
Vicci Bane
Cindy Barbour
Gerry Barnovski
Pauline Batzold
R.F. Bawe
Margaret Benjamin
Winston Berry
Fran Binder
Amy Birney
Liz Blackwell
G. Eileen Blaeske
Dulce Bohn
Susan Bohn
Barbara Boulton
Peggy Box
Melissa Boythe
Joanna Bradley
George and Lyn Breedon
Sandi Bresnick
Betsy Kuhn Brittain
Sally Brooks
Barbar Brouse
Marjorie I. Browning
Mary A. Brummett

Paula Bruno
Mrs. Michael Bryson
Gloria Burg
Tina Campo
Kristin Carlock
Kay Carlson
Kathleen B Chase
Ethel B. Clark
Diane Cleven
Jane Colan
Mrs. Fidelis Comaratta
Ivy Cooke
Jean Copeland
Leonie Crawford
Harold Creech
Carolyn Crozier
Gloria Cruickshanks
Mary Jo Daggit
Doris G. Davis
Pansy Delancey
Magda DeMauro
Jennifer DiMarzo
Dianne Downing
J.G. Dunning
Ada Eason
Valeria Wilmoth Edwards
Beverly Elwell
Susan Emery
Debbie Ennis
Frances P. Fiorentino
Judy Fitzgerald
Dianne Floyd
Peggy Follin

Charlotte Ford
Carolyn Foresta
Amy Froneberge
Brenda Gann
Anne Gatha
Anne Gildea
Janet M. Gillespie
Mary Virginia Glidewell
Susan W. Goodrich, Ph.D.
Tana Grills
Helen M. Guerino
Kendra Haden
Lena L. Hamrick
Vicki Hankins
Love Lindsey Hardaway
Sarah Hardaway
Peggie Harris
Peggy Abernathy Harris
Bill Harris
Susan Harris
Suzanne L. Haskell
Grace Hecht
Mrs. Robert A. Hellund
Martyn Hempston
Pamela Hempston
Doris T. Henderson
Laura Hendricks
Greta Hinson
Martie Hoftiezer
Sue Hood
Ann L. Horton
Tiffany E. Hoskins
Janis B. Howard
J. Breton Howle
Jim Humphrey
Tom Humphrey
Trish Humphrey
Lenore Hutter
Mark James
Dr. Marcy D. Johnson
Valerie Johnson

Frances Jones
Midge Jones
Millie S. Jones
Robb Jonsen
Allison Kellum
Laura Kershaw
Magz King
Susie Knable
Jules and Pat Krieger
Catherine M. Laferrara
Linda S. Lane
Sunny Lawson
Barbara R. Levy
Vicky Levy
Lyn Long
Nancy Lucaora
Margaret Lucas
Sue MacFarlan
Mary S. Maloney
Ursula May-Hertl
Elizabeth McCarty
Angela McCaslin
Karen McDonough
Pat McQuade
Beverly Miller
Sally Miller
Helen Milner
Susan Miskiewicz
Trish Morris
Caroline Moseley
Hennie Moss
Betty C. Muns
Lori Myers
Este Nemzer
Susan Millar Nicol
John Nolan
Anne Nolan
Stevie O'Hare
Brenda O'Shields
Lisa Parker
Jeanne Pastrnak

Heather & Steve Patton
Bryan and Carol Paul
Mandy Pearce
Becky Peters
Carol Pickard
Doug Pickler
Peggy Pielou
Alisa Pierce
Kelly Pillon
Betty W. Potts
Mary V. Powers
Erica Procton
Chris Puckett
Glenda Puleifer
Dixie C. Quinlan
Nina Rago
Josie Reed
Joan Regester
Doris Reynolds
Pat Rider
Gretchen and Robert Riesen
Thom and Joann Roberts
Carla Robinson
Gloria Robinson-Dawkins
Laura Rodgers
Francesca Rose
Ruth Rose
Annie & Robert Rosemond
Lisa Ross
Candi Ruppert
Michelle Saint-Dic
Emilie Samet
Penne Smith Sandbeck
Delores L. Sanders
Joyce Schlenz
Janet R. Seagrist
William Seagrist
Darla Seevers
Marie Shea
Nancy K. Simmons
Bonnie C. Smart

Lucretia E. Smith
Sarah L. Smith
Linda Soeder
Pat Stackman
L. Stanton
Francine Stedfast
Karen Stonis
Diane Stranczek
Jimmie R. Stroud
Dorothy Theckston
Judith H. Thoden
Elizabeth Thompson
Gracia Tilley
Michael Timpane
Patty Truax
Terri Tucker
Mary L. Turner
Jane Van Brimer
Kathy Van Dorp
Conny Walker
Joan E. Walker
Christine Walsh
Ruby Warlick
Win Weatherford
Anne Wehrley
Jo Ellen White
Maggie Wiedel
Helen Williams
Pam Williams
Maria Wilmoth
David Winfree
Susie Winterling
Jean Winters
Jeanne Marie Winters
Wanda C. Wood
Joan Worley
Sue Yeaw
Sue Young
Marissa Yuen
Beth Zierer

Contributors

CONTENTS

PRE

appetizers
soups
salads

Basil and Tomato Layered Cheese Torta

8 oz	Mascarpone cheese, softened
8 oz	cream cheese, softened
1 C	(6 oz) basil pesto, drain excess liquid
1 C	(6 oz) sun-dried tomato pesto, drain excess liquid
2 T	toasted pine nuts
	sprig of fresh basil

In mixer or with wooden spoon, blend softened cheeses until smooth. Line a 7-inch loaf pan with dampened cheese cloth with enough to hang over each side of the pan. With moist spatula, spread ⅓ cheese mixture in pan until evenly covered. Top with basil pesto, careful not to blend with cheese. Top with ⅓ cheese mixture by dropping small spoonfuls over previous layer and carefully spreading. Then spread the sun-dried tomato pesto and top with the remaining ⅓ of cheese mixture until evenly covered. Fold cheese cloth over top of cheese. Wrap in foil and refrigerate overnight. To serve, remove foil and cheese cloth carefully and invert onto serving platter. Top with pine nuts and fresh basil sprig. Serve at room temperature with plain crackers and French rounds.

Layered Seafood Appetizer

1 C	butter crackers, crushed
3 T	butter, melted
2	(8 oz) pkgs cream cheese, softened
3	eggs
¾ C	sour cream, divided
6-7 oz	crab meat, fresh or pasteurized (claw meat not recommended)
1 T	lemon juice
¼ C	green onions (reserve tops for garnish), chopped
3 T	green pepper, finely chopped
½ t	salt
¼ t	white pepper
¼ t	hot sauce or more to taste
	parsley
1 lb	shrimp, steamed in shells and peeled carefully

Preheat oven to 350°. Combine cracker crumbs and butter and mix thoroughly. Press into the bottom of a springform 8-inch pan. Bake 8-10 minutes, watching carefully to prevent burning. Remove from oven and set aside.

Reduce oven to 325°. Combine cream cheese, eggs, and ¼ cup sour cream. Beat until well blended. Add crab, lemon juice, onion, green pepper, white pepper, and hot sauce. Mix well and pour mixture into prepared crust. Bake 45-50 minutes or until middle is set and small cracks begin to appear. Remove from the oven and run a sharp knife around side of the pan, loosening cake. Cool on wire rack and carefully remove side of springform pan.

Place on a serving plate. Spread top evenly with remaining sour cream (can ice the sides as well and press with chopped parsley). Add shrimp in decorative pattern and sprinkle with parsley and finely chopped tops of green onions. Serve with crackers.

Brie with Rustic Fruit

2 T	unsalted butter
2	shallots, minced
1	small tart green apple, sliced with peel
6	dried figs, sliced
1	orange, skin zested
½	orange, juiced
⅓ C	walnuts, chopped
⅓ C	dried cherries
⅓ C	apple or guava jelly
2	(6") Brie rounds or 1 large

Melt butter in a sauté pan and sauté the minced shallots until soft. Add the apples, figs, orange zest, orange juice, walnuts, and cherries and simmer on low until the apples are just tender. Prepare the Brie round(s) by removing white rind from the top. Spoon topping over. Heat jelly in the microwave or in a small pan set over low until just melted. Brush jelly over fruit to add shine. Serve at room temperature with plain or flavored crackers.

Sun-dried Tomato Tapenade

3 oz	sun-dried tomatoes
	boiling water
3 T	olive oil
1 T	capers, drained
2 t	garlic, minced
1¼ t	lemon zest, finely grated
1 t	fresh lemon juice
¼ t	herbes de Provence or pinches of thyme, basil, and oregano
	salt

Place the tomatoes in a heatproof bowl and cover with boiling water. Set aside until softened, about 2 minutes. Drain the tomatoes and pat dry. In a food processor, add softened tomatoes and remaining ingredients. Process to a very course purée. Add additional oil if desired. Best served at room temperature. Delicious served on or with Brie.

Makes about 1½ cups.

MAKE AHEAD: Tapenade can be made up to one week ahead. Keep covered and refrigerated. Bring tapenade to room temperature before serving.

Green Olive Tapenade

1	(7 oz) jar cured pitted green olives, well drained
1½ t	anchovy paste
1	large garlic clove
1 t	capers, rinsed and drained
¼ C	olive oil
1 t	fresh lemon juice
⅛ t	cayenne pepper
	toasted bread slices

Combine olives, anchovy paste, garlic, and capers in processor and purée until smooth. With machine running, slowly add oil and process until mixture resembles smooth paste, occasionally scraping down sides of work bowl. Mix in lemon juice and cayenne. Transfer to bowl. Delicious served on or with Brie.

Makes about 1⅓ cups.

MAKE AHEAD: This tapenade can be prepared up to 1 week ahead. Keep covered and refrigerated until ready to use. Allow to come to room temperature before serving.

Roasted Pepper and Artichoke Tapenade

1	(7 oz) jar or fresh roasted red bell peppers, drained and coarsely chopped
1	(14 oz) can artichoke hearts, drained and coarsely chopped
⅓ C	fresh parsley, stems removed
½ C	freshly grated Parmesan cheese
3 T	olive oil
¼ C	capers, drained
2	garlic cloves, chopped
1½ T	fresh lemon juice
	salt and pepper

Combine all ingredients in processor. Process using on/off turns until well blended and finely chopped. Do not purée. Season to taste with salt and pepper. Serve on French rounds or crackers.

MAKE AHEAD: The flavor is best when prepared a day ahead. Cover and refrigerate.

Makes 1¾ cups.

INSPIRATION: Leftover tapenade is delicious mixed with hot pasta.

Tuna and Watercress Tapenade

1	(6 oz) can albacore tuna, well drained
⅓ C	mayonnaise
4 oz	cream cheese, room temperature
2 T	fresh lemon juice
¼ t	fresh ground white pepper
2 C	watercress leaves (1 bunch)
4	green onions and tops, chopped
2½ T	small capers, drained and rinsed
dash	hot sauce
	salt

In a food processor, combine tuna, mayonnaise, cream cheese, lemon juice, and pepper. Blend until smooth. Add remaining ingredients and pulse only until well-blended.

Cover and refrigerate for at least 2 hours or overnight. Serve with plain crackers and celery sticks.

Spicy Glazed Pecans

½ C	sugar
3 T	water
⅞ t	salt
½ t	cayenne pepper
3 C	pecan halves

Preheat oven to 350°. Butter a heavy large baking sheet. Combine sugar, water, salt, and pepper in heavy small saucepan. Stir over medium heat until sugar dissolves. Boil 2 minutes. Add pecans and stir until pecans are coated with mixture, about 1 minute. Transfer pecans to prepared sheet, spreading evenly. Bake until pecans are just beginning to brown, about 13 minutes. Transfer to a sheet of foil or waxed paper and quickly separate pecans with a fork. Cool completely. Store in an airtight container up to 1 week.

INSPIRATION: Cooled pecans may also be frozen. Serve along with a tray of cookies. Also add to green salads and our Waldorf Salad with Dried Cherries (see Index).

Cumin and Cayenne Spiced Cashews

1	egg white
1 lb	salted and roasted cashews
⅓ C	sugar
2 t	cumin
2 t	coarse (kosher) salt
1½ t	cayenne pepper

Preheat oven to 250°. In a medium bowl, whisk the egg white with 1 tablespoon water until foamy. Add the cashews and toss to coat. Transfer the nuts to a strainer and let drain for at least 2 minutes. In a bowl, combine sugar, cumin, salt, and cayenne pepper. Add the nuts and toss thoroughly to coat. On a large baking sheet with sides, spread the nuts out in a single layer. Bake for 40 minutes. Stir with spatula and spread out again. Reduce temperature to 200° and bake for 30 minutes more. Using a spatula, loosen the nuts from the baking sheet and let cool on sheet. Let nuts cool completely and get crisp before storing. They will keep up to a week in an airtight container.

Appetizers

Hot Artichoke Dip

1	(14 oz) can artichoke hearts, drained and chopped
1¼ C	light mayonnaise
2	(4.5 oz) cans green chiles, drained and diced
4 oz	Monterey jack cheese, shredded
⅓ C	Parmesan cheese, grated
	hot sauce
	cayenne
	additional grated Parmesan cheese

Preheat oven to 325°. In a medium bowl, mix artichokes, mayonnaise, green chiles, Monterey jack cheese, and ⅓ cup Parmesan cheese. Season to taste with hot sauce and cayenne. Spread mixture into a shallow 1½-quart baking dish. Sprinkle with additional Parmesan cheese.

MAKE AHEAD: Could be prepared the day before. Cover and refrigerate.

Bake uncovered for 30 minutes until bubbly. Serve with corn or tortilla chips or plain crackers.

Crab-Artichoke Dip

1½ t	oil
½	medium red bell pepper, diced
1	(14 oz) can artichoke hearts, drained and chopped
½ C	mayonnaise
½ C	Parmesan cheese, grated
1½ t	Worcestershire sauce
1 T	pickled jalapeño, finely chopped
1½ t	fresh lemon juice
8 oz	fresh or pasteurized crab meat
⅓ C	sliced almonds as a topping (optional)

Sauté red bell pepper in oil for 3 minutes. Add remaining ingredients except crab and almonds. Mix well. Gently blend in crab. Season to taste. Top with almonds if desired. Can refrigerate at this point. Bake 375° for 30 minutes or until brown and bubbly.

INSPIRATION: Dip is a great stuffing for mushroom caps.

Crab Dip

3 oz	cream cheese, softened
¼ C	mayonnaise
¼ C	sour cream
1	(6 oz) can crab meat, high quality, drained well
¼ C	onion, minced
1 t	fresh lemon juice
⅛ t	hot pepper sauce
	salt and pepper to taste

Preheat oven to 350°. Beat cream cheese until smooth; add other ingredients, blending well. Bake at 350° for 30 minutes, in a small oven proof dish, such as an au gratin dish. Serve hot with corn chips and plain crackers.

Curry Cheese Dip

1 C	sharp Cheddar cheese, shredded
1 C	mayonnaise
1 C	onion, chopped
¼ C	green pepper, chopped
½ t	dry dill weed
¼-½ t	curry powder

Mix ingredients and put in oven proof bowl. Bake at 325° for 30-40 minutes.
Serve with corn chips and crackers.

Roasted Red Bell Pepper Dip

3	large red bell peppers, roasted, peeled, and seeded
1	green onion, cut into 1" pieces
1½ T	lemon juice
1 C	whipped cream cheese, room temperature
	baguette slices

Place roasted and peeled peppers, green onions, and lemon juice in food processor and purée. Add the cream cheese and pulse to mix. Transfer to a bowl, cover, and refrigerate for at least 1 hour. Can store in refrigerator for 2 days. Serve with baguette slices.

Makes 2 cups.

Vidalia Onion Dip

4 C	sweet Vidalia onions, chopped fine
3 C	Swiss cheese, shredded
2 C	regular or light mayonnaise

Mix ingredients. Put into a 2-quart casserole dish and bake at 350° for 25-35 minutes until bubbly and brown. Serve with French rounds or water crackers.

Bean Dip

1	(15 oz) can white or yellow corn
1	(15 oz) can black eye peas
1	(15 oz) can black beans
½	red pepper, diced
½	green pepper, diced
1	small red onion, diced
2	cans Rotel, drained
1	small bottle Italian dressing

Drain corn, peas, and beans. Add red and green peppers, onion, and drained tomatoes to bean mixture. Add Italian dressing and mix well. Chill until served. Use corn chips for dipping.

Black Bean Hummus

1	(15 oz) can black beans, drained
2 T	lemon juice
2	cloves garlic
1½ T	tahini
1 T	olive oil
¼ C	sweet onion, chopped
¼ t	salt and pepper

Place all ingredients in a blender or food processor and blend until there is a thick consistency. Serve chilled with toasted pita bread.

INSPIRATION: To toast pita bread, preheat oven to 450° and lightly brush pita with olive oil. Place pita on a foil covered baking sheet and toast in oven 5-7 minutes or until pita is lightly browned.

Mango Spread

2	ripe mangoes, in chunks
1	ripe peach, in chunks
1	jalapeño pepper, seeded and finely minced
	season to taste with lemon juice, pinch of salt, white pepper, and cayenne (if jalapeño mild)
8 oz	block light cream cheese

Purée the mangoes and peach in a food processor. Add jalapeño and season to taste. Pour over the cream cheese and serve with crackers.

Strawberry Salsa

4 T	olive oil
2 T	balsamic vinegar
½ t	salt
1 pt	fresh strawberries, coarsely chopped
8	green onions, chopped
2 pts	cherry tomatoes, chopped
½ C	fresh cilantro, chopped
¼ t	black pepper

Whisk together oil, vinegar, and salt in large bowl. Add strawberries and remaining ingredients, tossing to coat. Chill at least 1 hour. Serve with tortilla chips.

Makes 6 cups.

INSPIRATION: Serve as a relish with pork or chicken.

Pub Cheese Spread

8 oz	Cheddar cheese, grated
8 oz	cream cheese, softened
½ C	beer (strong flavor)
1 t	dry mustard
½ t	cayenne pepper
1 t	prepared horseradish
1 T	parsley, minced

Put all ingredients, except parsley, into blender or food processor. Mix. Spoon into small dish. Top with parsley. Serve cold with crackers and vegetables.

Spicy Tomato Goat Cheese Fondue

1 C	marinara sauce, mild flavored
¾ C	stewed tomatoes
½ t	Italian seasoning
½–¾ t	hot sauce
¼ C	red wine
3 oz	goat cheese, ½" thick slice or a log

Combine sauce and tomatoes in saucepan over medium heat. Season to taste with seasoning, hot sauce, and red wine. Simmer to heat. Place goat cheese in center of baking dish. Pour sauce around cheese and bake at 350° until cheese is warm. Garnish with parsley flakes and serve on toast points or French rounds.

Gruyere Puffs

1 C	Swiss or Gruyere cheese, grated
1 C	water
5 T	butter
1 t	salt
¼ t	freshly ground pepper
¼ t	freshly ground nutmeg
1 C	flour
5	large eggs, at room temperature

Preheat oven to 425°. Grate cheese. In a medium-sized saucepan bring the water, butter, salt, pepper, and nutmeg to a boil. When butter has melted, remove from heat. Add all the flour to butter and water mixture and beat with a wooden spoon until mixture leaves sides of pan clean. Add cheese and beat until incorporated. Beat in 4 of the eggs one by one until thoroughly absorbed. Beat until mixture is smooth, shiny, and firm. Drop by small spoonfuls onto a greased cookie sheet. Beat remaining egg with ½ tablespoon water, and then brush tops of uncooked puffs with egg wash. Bake in upper third of the oven for about 20 minutes or until golden and doubled in size. Remove from oven and serve. You'll have about 3 dozen. This recipe can be easily halved.

Parmesan Rounds

8 oz	cream cheese, softened
½ C	butter, softened
½ C	light mayonnaise
4-6	green onions, finely chopped
	Parmesan cheese, freshly grated
	French rounds

Combine cream cheese, butter, mayonnaise, and green onions. Spread mixture on French rounds covering to edges and dip into Parmesan.

MAKE AHEAD: At this point, rounds can be frozen.

Preheat broiler. Broil until bubbly and golden. This only takes a little time so watch carefully. Serve immediately.

Appetizers

Mushroom Crustades

3 T	butter
3 T	shallots, finely chopped
½ lb	mushrooms, chopped
3 T	flour
½ C	heavy cream
½ t	salt
⅛ t	cayenne pepper
1 T	parsley, chopped
1½ T	chives
½ t	lemon juice
2 T	Parmesan cheese
4 T	butter
24	crustades or small pastry shells

Heat 3 tablespoons butter and sauté shallots. Add mushrooms and sauté until all liquid evaporates. Remove from heat and sprinkle the flour over the mixture; stir thoroughly. Add heavy cream. Blend well and return to heat, bringing mixture to a boil. Lower to simmer and cook until thick. Remove from heat and add salt, cayenne, parsley, chives, and lemon juice. Taste for additional seasoning.

MAKE AHEAD: Mushroom mixture can be prepared a day ahead and refrigerated.

Preheat oven to 350°. Mound filling into crustades (or small pastry shells). Sprinkle with cheese and dot with butter. Arrange on cookie sheet and bake for 10 minutes. Place briefly under broiler. Best if served hot.

Marinated Mushrooms

3 lb	fresh white mushrooms, sliced or quartered
1 t	salt
1	lemon, juiced
1 C	red wine vinegar
1 C	water
1	(4 oz) jar small green olives
2	garlic cloves, whole
3 t	parsley, chopped
½ t	salt
¼ t	pepper
⅛ t	oregano
½ t	olive oil

Put mushrooms in a large saucepan. Cover with water, add salt and lemon juice. Bring just to a boil, simmer 5 minutes. Drain. Place in a nonreactive bowl, add wine vinegar and water, marinate overnight in the refrigerator. Drain and save liquid. Add the remaining ingredients and enough marinade to cover the mushrooms. Cover and refrigerate for 2-3 days.

Smoked Salmon Rolls

12	slices wood-smoked salmon 4 x 2½" each
½ C	cream cheese, softened
¼ C	sour cream
2 T	fresh chives (or fresh basil or dill), chopped
	white pepper

Combine the cream cheese and sour cream until smooth. Place 1 salmon slice on work surface and spread with about 2 teaspoons of cream cheese mixture. Sprinkle with ½ teaspoon chives and freshly ground white pepper. Starting at one of the short ends, roll up salmon enclosing the filling. Repeat with remaining salmon. Cover and chill for up to 6 hours. Before serving, cut each roll crosswise into 2-3 slices depending on desired serving size.

Appetizers

Shrimp Vinaigrette Wrapped in Snow Peas

1 lb	(21-30) large shrimp, cleaned and cooked
15-20	snow peas

Vinaigrette

½ C	olive oil
3 T	white wine vinegar
3 T	Dijon mustard
1 T	shallots, chopped
1 t	ginger, finely minced
1 T	fresh dill, chopped
	pinch of sugar
	salt and pepper to taste

Place cooked shrimp in a glass or steel bowl. Mix vinaigrette ingredients in a covered jar. Shake well and pour over shrimp. Coat well, cover bowl, and refrigerate up to 1 day, tossing several times. String the peas and blanch in boiling water for 30 seconds. Drain and immerse peas in iced water. Drain again. Split the peas lengthwise so that you have 30-40 separate halves. Wrap a pea pod half around each shrimp and fasten by piercing with a natural wood toothpick. Serve cold or at room temperature.

Appetizers

New Orleans Style Barbequed Shrimp

2 lbs	(31-40 count) peeled and deveined tail-on shrimp
1 C	butter
1 C	vegetable oil
1 T	garlic, finely minced
4	bay leaves, crushed
2 T	rosemary leaves, crushed
1 T	paprika
1 T	coarse ground pepper
½	lemon, sliced in rings
¾ T	dried basil
¾ T	dried oregano
¾ T	salt
½ t	cayenne pepper

In a large, heavy skillet, heat butter and oil. Sauté garlic until lightly brown. Add remaining ingredients, except shrimp. Cook, stirring until it comes to a boil. Cover and simmer for 5 minutes, stirring frequently. Remove cover and add shrimp, one pound at a time. Cook over medium heat until the shrimp change from translucent to opaque in color. Remove shrimp and place in a deep dish. Let the sauce cool. Pour cooled sauce over shrimp and let soak up to 5 hours in the refrigerator. Warm up dish right before serving. Serve with good French bread and plenty of napkins!

Thom's Spicy Chicken Wings

14	chicken drummettes or 10 chicken wings
2 T	Dijon mustard
2	eggs, slightly beaten
1 T	water
1 C	plain dry breadcrumbs
1 T	lemon pepper
1 t	cayenne pepper

Preheat oven to 350°. Combine eggs, mustard, and water in a flat dish. In another flat dish toss breadcrumbs, lemon pepper, and cayenne pepper. Wash and thoroughly dry the chicken. Dip chicken in the egg mixture and coat well, and then dredge in breadcrumb mixture to make a thick crust. Bake in oven on a cookie sheet, lightly sprayed with oil, for 45 minutes or until they are browned and cooked through. Serve with blue cheese dressing and celery sticks.

Appetizers

Josephina's Appetizer

1	loaf French bread, sliced horizontally
1 T	butter, softened
2 T	mayonnaise
1	small jar sliced jalapeño peppers, or to taste
1 lb	Monterey jack cheese, grated

Preheat oven 350°. Line cookie sheet with foil. Spread butter on both sides of bread. Mix Monterey jack cheese with mayonnaise. Spread jalapeños evenly over both sides of buttered bread. Spread cheese mixture over jalapeños. Bake for 20-25 minutes until cheese is light brown. Cool 5 minutes before cutting.

Party Ham Rolls

3 pkgs	small rolls or biscuits
¾ lb	Swiss cheese, shredded
1½ lb	ham, sliced thin
Sauce	
2	sticks butter
1	medium onion, chopped
1 t	Worcestershire sauce
1 T	prepared mustard
1 T	poppy seeds

Prepare sauce: Melt butter, add other ingredients and sauté until onion is done and sauce thickens. Slice rolls. Spread sauce on bottom of rolls, add ham, and then shredded Swiss cheese. Cover with top of roll. Tightly wrap in aluminum foil and bake in preheated 350° oven for about 20 minutes. Serve hot.

INSPIRATION: You can freeze prepared rolls, then thaw, heat, and serve.

Bruschetta

6	ripe tomatoes, diced
2 T	olive oil
8	kalamata olives, diced finely
8	large fresh basil leaves, chopped
2 t	balsamic vinegar
1	small garlic clove, crushed
dash	salt
	ground pepper
	French rounds

Combine all the ingredients. Let stand 1 hour at room temperature. Adjust seasoning. Serve tomato mixture on French rounds.

Always serve at room temperature.

PRE

appetizers

soups

salads

Cantaloupe Soup

3-5	fresh peaches, peeled and chopped
4 oz	crushed pineapple, in its own juices
4 oz	pineapple chunks, in its own juices
8 oz	unsweetened orange juice
4 T	lemon juice
⅛ t	nutmeg
⅛ t	cinnamon
1 t	vanilla
1	medium to large cantaloupe, cut into cubes
	chopped basil for garnish

Place chopped peaches into a blender along with the pineapple, orange juice, lemon juice, nutmeg, cinnamon, and vanilla. Pulse to blend coarsely. Add cantaloupe; start with 1 cup until you have a decidedly cantaloupe flavor, rather than a pineapple taste. Refrigerate overnight so all the flavors blend together. Stir before serving. Garnish with chopped basil.

INSPIRATION: This unusual chilled soup is delicious served for breakfast, lunch or as an appetizer before dinner.

Soups

Cucumber Vichyssoise

5 C	(2 lb) russet potatoes, peeled and cut into ½" pieces
2 T	butter
¼ C	shallots, chopped
4 C	leeks (about 4)
4 C	chicken broth
2 C	water
2 t	salt
½ t	pepper
3 C	cucumber, peeled, seeded, and chopped
½ C	sour cream
3 T	lemon juice
½ C	chives, chopped

Trim the leeks so only the white and pale green parts remain. Cut the leeks lengthwise down the middle and clean under cold running water. Slice. In a large soup pot, melt the butter on medium-low. Add the leeks and shallots, cook stirring occasionally for about 15 minutes until soft but not brown. Add the potatoes, broth, water, salt, and pepper. Bring to a boil, reduce heat and cover. Simmer until potatoes are tender.

Working in batches, purée the soup thoroughly not to leave any lumps. During the last batch, add the cucumbers, sour cream, and lemon juice. Season to taste. Add the chives. Chill at least 6 hours or overnight. Adjust seasoning. Serve cold, garnish with additional chives and a spoonful of sour cream.

INSPIRATION: Serve as potato soup, omit the cucumbers and heat thoroughly. Just before serving add sour cream and lemon juice. Do not boil. Garnish with chives.

Soups

Cold Avocado and Green Chili Soup

1	small garlic clove
¼ C	sweet onion
1	ripe avocado, pitted, peeled, and quartered
1	(4 oz) can green chilies, drained
1	tomatillo, husked and quartered (or lemon juice to add tartness)
2 C	chicken stock, chilled
¾ C	light sour cream
½ t	salt
⅛ t	white pepper

In a food processor or blender, finely chop garlic and onion. Add avocado, chilies, tomatillo, and chicken stock and blend until smooth. Blend in sour cream, salt, and pepper. Check seasonings. Serve immediately or cover and refrigerate for 2 hours. Garnish with fried tortilla strips or fresh tomato salsa.

Soups

Corn Soup

6	ears corn (about 6 cups of kernels)
4 T	unsalted butter
2	shallots, finely chopped
2 t	flour
1 C	homemade or canned chicken stock
1 C	half & half
½ t	salt, or more to taste
½ t	freshly ground pepper
2 T	roughly chopped fresh flat-leaf parsley or basil
1 oz	Parmesan cheese, grated, plus extra for garnish

Using a chef's knife, remove kernels from cobs into a bowl. Using dull side of knife, scrape milk and pulp from cobs; add to bowl. Heat butter in a medium saucepan over medium heat. When melted and bubbling, add shallots. Cook, stirring, until soft and translucent. Add corn kernels, corn milk, pulp, and flour. Cook, stirring, 1 minute. Stir in chicken stock. Turn heat to high; cook until liquid is reduced by half, about 3 minutes. Add half & half; cook until mixture is thick and creamy, about 4 minutes more. Remove from heat; stir in salt, pepper, herbs, and cheese. Divide among four bowls. Garnish with Parmesan.

Soups

Lemony Squash Soup

1½ lb	yellow squash, large seeds removed
1	large sweet onion, chopped
2-4	cloves garlic, chopped
2 T	fresh thyme
½ C	fresh cilantro, chopped
⅛ t	red pepper flakes
1	lemon, juiced
	salt and pepper to taste
2	(14 oz) cans vegetable broth
1½ C	water

Sauté squash, onions, and garlic in 2 tablespoons olive oil until soft. Add thyme, ¼ cup cilantro, pepper flakes, salt, pepper, and lemon. Cook for several minutes. Add water and broth and simmer about 10 minutes. Ladle half of the mixture into a blender and purée. Add the purée back to pot and simmer for 5 minutes and add ¼ cup chopped cilantro. Serve garnished with additional cilantro.

Curried Sweet Potato & Pear Soup with Roquefort Croutons

1	onion, chopped
2 T	unsalted butter
1½ lbs	sweet potatoes, peeled and cut into 1" pieces
1½ lbs	pears (about 4), peeled, cored and chopped
5½ C	chicken broth
1 C	dry white wine
2 t	curry powder
1	bay leaf
6	¾" diagonal slices cut from a baguette
6 oz	Roquefort cheese, softened

In a soup pot sauté onion in butter over moderately low heat, stirring, until softened. Add sweet potatoes, pears, broth, wine, curry powder, and bay leaf and simmer 15-20 minutes, or until potatoes are very tender. Discard bay leaf and in a blender purée soup in batches. Return puréed soup to pot and season with salt and pepper.

Preheat broiler. On a baking sheet lightly toast both sides of bread slices about 3 inches from heat until golden. Spread about 1 ounce Roquefort on one side of each toast and broil until melted. Cool toasts and with a sharp knife cut into 1-inch croutons. Heat soup until hot and serve with croutons.

Soups

Harvest Squash and Zucchini Soup

3 C	butternut squash, peeled and cubed
3 C	zucchini, peeled and cubed
2	medium potatoes, peeled and cubed
1	large onion, sliced
2 C	chicken stock
2 T	fresh parsley, chopped
2	cloves garlic, chopped
1-2 t	dried basil
¾ C	milk (optional)

In a large saucepan, combine squash, zucchini, potatoes, onion, chicken stock, parsley, and garlic. Cover and simmer, stirring occasionally for 45 minutes or until vegetables are tender. If stock simmers down add more water to reach original level. In food processor or blender, puree mixture in batches; return to saucepan and add basil and milk (if using), heat until hot.

Soups

Pumpkin Mushroom Soup

½ lb	fresh mushrooms, sliced
½ C	onion, chopped
2 T	butter
2 T	flour
1 T	curry powder
3 C	chicken stock
1	(16 oz) can pumpkin
1 T	honey
dash	nutmeg
	salt and pepper to taste
1 C	heavy cream or half & half

Sauté mushrooms and onions in butter. Add flour and curry powder and stir until bubbly. Gradually add the stock; stir until mixed. Bring to a simmer. Reduce heat, add pumpkin, honey, and other seasonings. Stir while cooking, approximately 15 minutes. Add cream and heat through without boiling. Top with a dollop of sour cream if desired.

Soups

Wild Mushroom Soup

SERVES
8

1 oz	dried cepes, morels, or chanterelles
¾ C	Madeira wine
1	stick butter
2 C	yellow onions, finely chopped
2 lb	fresh mushrooms
	salt and pepper to taste
4 C	chicken stock

Rinse the dried mushrooms well in a sieve under cold running water and soak in Madeira for 1 hour, stirring occasionally.

Melt butter in soup pot. Add onions and cook covered over low heat until tender, about 15 minutes. Clean mushrooms, slice thin and add to soup pot. Season with salt and pepper and cook uncovered over low heat, stirring frequently for 15 minutes. Carefully lift dried mushrooms from Madeira with slotted spoon and transfer to soup pot. Let Madeira settle, pour carefully through cheesecloth into soup pot. Add chicken stock and bring to a boil. Reduce heat, cover and simmer for 45 minutes or until dried mushrooms are very tender.

Soups

Vegetable Brie Soup

SERVES
6

8 oz	Brie cheese
½ C	butter
½ C	celery, finely chopped
½ C	carrots, finely chopped
½ C	onion, finely chopped
½ C	flour
2 C	chicken broth
1	bay leaf
½ t	dried thyme or 1-2 t fresh thyme
½ C	heavy cream

Garnish

chives or parsley, finely chopped
carrots, shredded

Cut rind from Brie and discard; set cheese aside. Sauté vegetables in butter in a heavy saucepan over medium heat. Stir frequently. Add flour and mix in well; allow to bubble 3-4 minutes, stirring constantly. Gradually add broth, bay leaf, and thyme. Cook, stirring constantly, until mixture thickens. Add cheese and stir until smooth. Pour in cream and stir well. Place soup in bowls and garnish.

Soups

Chili-Cheese Chowder

2	bacon slices
1 C	carrot, chopped
1 C	poblano chilies (or red and green bell peppers), seeded and chopped
1 C	onion, chopped
2 T	jalapeño peppers, seeded and minced
½ t	cumin, ground
3	garlic cloves, minced
2	(14 oz) cans chicken broth
4 C	baking potato, peeled and diced
½ t	salt
⅓ C	flour
2½ C	1% low-fat milk (can use 1 cup of fat-free half & half)
¾ C	(3 oz) Monterey jack cheese with jalapeño peppers, shredded
½ C	(2 oz) sharp Cheddar cheese, shredded (optional)
⅔ C	green onions, sliced

Cook bacon in a Dutch oven over medium-high heat until crisp. Remove bacon from pan, reserving 1 tablespoon drippings in pan. Crumble bacon; set aside. Add carrot, poblano, onion, jalapeño peppers, cumin, and garlic to drippings in pan; sauté 10 minutes or until browned. Stir in the broth, scraping pan to loosen browned bits. Add potato and salt. Bring to a boil; cover, reduce heat, and simmer 25 minutes or until potato is tender.

Lightly spoon flour into a dry measuring cup; level with a knife. Combine flour and milk in a small bowl, stirring with a whisk. Add to pan. Cook over medium heat until thick (about 12 minutes), stirring frequently. Remove from heat. Add cheeses, stirring until cheeses melt. Ladle into soup bowls; top with green onions and crumbled bacon.

Soups

White Bean Soup

1 t	olive oil
1	large red onion, cut into chunks
1	celery stalk, cut into chunks
1	garlic clove, smashed and chopped
1½ C	dry navy beans (soaked overnight)
1	(28 oz) can tomatoes with juice
4 C	chicken stock

Season to taste: thyme, oregano, basil, parsley, salt, pepper

Heat oil in large pot over medium-high heat. Add onions, celery, and garlic. Cook for 5 minutes. Add beans and remaining ingredients; mix well. Season to taste, cover, and bring to a boil. Reduce heat to low and continue cooking covered for 3 hours or until beans are tender. Stir every 15 minutes. Serve hot.

Soups

Andouille Sausage Soup

	olive oil
8 oz	fresh mushrooms, sliced thin
2	medium onions, slivered
1 lb	andouille sausage, cut into ¼" pieces
4	(14 oz) cans chicken broth, plus 1 can of water
1½ C	carrots, sliced thin
2 t	garlic, minced
½ t	tarragon
1 t	pepper, coarsely ground
2-3	bay leaves
3	cans white cannelli, northern, or navy beans, drained and rinsed.

Sauté mushrooms and onions in small amount of olive oil until lightly browned. Add sausage, chicken broth, water, carrots, and seasonings. Simmer until carrots are tender. Remove bay leaves. Add beans. Cook on low for 10-15 minutes.

INSPIRATION: For a heartier soup: add cubed potatoes, fresh green beans (cut in 1" pieces), sliced squash or zucchini or black beans.

Soups

Tortellini and White Bean Soup

3	garlic cloves, minced
1	large onion, chopped
1	red bell pepper, chopped
1½ t	Italian seasoning
1 T	olive oil
3	(14 oz) cans chicken broth
1	(16 oz) can navy beans, drained
1	(14 oz) can chopped tomatoes
1	(14 oz) can artichoke hearts, drained and quartered
1	(8 oz) pkg dried cheese filled tortellini, cooked; or 9 oz refrigerated tortellini, cooked
2 C	fresh spinach, coarsely chopped
	Parmesan cheese for garnish

Sauté garlic, onion, pepper, and Italian seasoning in hot oil in a large Dutch oven over medium heat. Add broth, beans, tomatoes and artichokes. Bring to a boil, reduce heat and simmer 2 minutes. Add cooked tortellini and spinach. Simmer for 5 more minutes. Serve and sprinkle with shredded Parmesan cheese.

INSPIRATION: This soup is also delicious without the tortellini.

Sweet and Sour Chicken Soup

SERVES
6

⅓ C	onion, finely chopped
3	garlic cloves, minced
½ t	fresh ginger, grated
6 C	chicken stock
1½ T	rice vinegar
2 T	low-sodium soy sauce
½ t	salt
⅛ t	ground white pepper
1½ C	shiitake mushroom caps, thinly sliced
1½ C	cooked chicken, shredded
2 C	spinach leaves, thinly sliced
1½ oz	somen (wheat noodles) or angel hair pasta, uncooked

In a large soup pot, sauté onion and garlic in 2 teaspoons olive oil for 3 minutes. Add ginger for 30 seconds. Add chicken stock through mushrooms, bring to a boil. Cover, reduce heat, and simmer 30 minutes. Stir in chicken, spinach, and noodles; cook for 5 minutes.

Soups

61

Oyster Soup

2	(½ pt) containers oysters
¼ C	onion, chopped
4 T	butter
4 T	flour
2	(10½ oz) cans beef broth, double strength
2	cans full of water
½ C	half & half

Drain oysters reserving juices. Melt butter, sauté onions for 3 minutes until tender. Stir in flour and cook over low heat about 2 minutes stirring constantly. Slowly whisk in oyster juices, beef broth, and water. Cook while stirring until liquid comes to a boil. Season to taste with salt and pepper. Just before serving, return to a boil, add half & half and oysters. Cook briefly just until oysters curl. Adjust seasoning. Serve at once.

INSIGHT: When adding a liquid such as stock or milk to a roux (butter and flour mixture), heat the liquid in the microwave before gradually whisking into the roux. This will reduce the amount of time it takes to thicken the roux.

Seafood Stew

2 T	olive oil
1¼ C	onion, chopped
1-2 T	garlic, chopped
1 T	dried oregano
1½ t	fennel seeds (optional)
2½ C	tomatoes with added purée, crushed
1 C	bottled clam juice
1 C	chicken stock
¾ C	dry white wine
1 lb	uncooked large shrimp, peeled, and deveined
1	(½ pt) container oysters or 6 oz firm white fish cut into 1" pieces
¼ C	fresh basil, chopped
	cayenne pepper
	salt and pepper

Heat olive oil in soup pot over medium heat. Add onion, garlic, oregano, and fennel seeds and sauté until onion is tender, about 8 minutes. Add tomatoes, clam juice, chicken stock, white wine, and liquid from oysters. Increase heat and boil until slightly thickened, about 15 minutes. Add seafood. Reduce heat and simmer 2 minutes. Mix in fresh basil and simmer until shrimp are just opaque in center, about 2 minutes longer. Season stew to taste with cayenne, salt, and pepper.

Soups

Rotisserie Chicken Stock

4	rotisserie chicken carcasses
2	onions, quartered
2	carrots, quartered
4	large celery stalks with leaves, cut into 2" chunks
2	bay leaves
4	fresh thyme sprigs
1 T	whole peppercorns
1 t	salt
3 qts	water

Place all ingredients into a large stock pot. Bring to a boil and remove foam that rises to the surface. Reduce heat and simmer, partially covered for 2 hours.

Strain the liquid carefully, pressing gently on the bones and vegetables to extract the liquid. Refrigerate the liquid for several hours or overnight until the fat has risen to the surface. Scrape off fat before using stock.

Makes about 2 quarts of stock.

INSPIRATION: Get in the habit of freezing the carcasses from your purchased rotisserie chickens (all parts, including skin if desired). When you have accumulated a few chickens, thaw in refrigerator and proceed with stock recipe. It is convenient to freeze stock in 1 cup increments for use in recipes.

Soups

PRE

appetizers

soups

salads

Belgian Endive, Apple, and Almond Salad

Salad

1	tart green apple, cut into ½" cubes
2	Belgian endives, thinly sliced crosswise
⅓ C	almonds, toasted and sliced

Dressing

2 T	salad oil
1 T	lemon juice
1 t	garlic, minced
	salt and pepper to taste

Mix apple, endives, and almonds together in a bowl. Mix the dressing and pour on salad. Toss thoroughly and serve.

Fresh Orange and Date Salad

SERVES
4-6

½ C	dried dates
¼ C	salad oil or light olive oil
1½ T	lemon juice
	salt
2	juicy oranges
	lettuce leaves, Boston or leaf
	walnuts, toasted and chopped

Cover dates with boiling water and leave to soften and plump up for about 10 minutes (This does not need to be done if the dates are already plump and soft). Then drain dates thoroughly, stone them and cut into small pieces. In a bowl, beat oil and lemon juice together with a pinch of salt. Add dates and toss with a fork until well mixed.

Peel oranges, removing every scrap of white pith. Cut them horizontally into thin slices, picking and discarding seeds as you come across them. Line a serving platter or bowl with lettuce leaves. Arrange orange slices on them and spoon dates and dressing over the top. Sprinkle with a few chopped walnuts and serve.

Salads & Dressings

Waldorf Salad with Dried Cherries

½ C	light mayonnaise
3 T	light sour cream
2 T	fresh lemon juice
1 t	sugar
4	Granny Smith apples, cored, cut into ½" cubes
1⅓ C	celery, very thinly sliced
1⅓ C	red seedless grapes, halved
⅔ C	dried tart cherries
	romaine lettuce leaves
	Spicy Glazed Pecans (see Index)

Whisk mayonnaise, sour cream, lemon juice, and sugar in a large bowl. Add apples, celery, grapes, and cherries; toss. Season with salt and pepper. Arrange lettuce on platter; spoon salad over. Top salad with spiced pecans

INSPIRATION: Add chicken for a delicious chicken Waldorf salad.

INSIGHT: This simple apple salad was created in 1896, not by a chef but by the maitre d' hotel at the luxurious Waldorf-Astoria Hotel in New York. The original version of this salad contained only apples, celery, and mayonnaise. Many variations have since evolved – some with raisins and chopped nuts. This one has green apples, red seedless grapes, and dried cherries.

Salads & Dressings

Blueberry Spinach Salad

½ C	light olive oil
¼ C	raspberry vinegar
2 t	Dijon mustard
1 t	sugar
½ t	salt
10 oz	fresh spinach, torn
4 oz	blue cheese, crumbled
1 C	fresh blueberries, washed & dried
½ C	pecans, toasted and chopped

In a jar, combine oil, vinegar, Dijon, sugar, and salt and shake well. In a large salad bowl, toss the spinach, with half of the cheese, half of the blueberries, and half of the pecans. Add enough dressing to coat and toss gently. Garnish salad with remaining cheese, fruit, and pecans.

INSPIRATION: If fresh blueberries are out of season, use dried blueberries, cranberries, or cherries, or other fresh fruit.

Salads & Dressings

Spinach Strawberry Salad with Sesame Seed Dressing

Salad

24 oz	fresh baby spinach
1 pt	fresh strawberries, sliced

Dressing

½ C	oil
¼ C	cider vinegar
¼ C	sugar
2 T	sesame seeds
1 T	onion, minced
¼ t	Worcestershire sauce
¼ t	paprika

For dressing put all ingredients except oil in a blender. With blender running add oil in a slow steady stream until completely mixed and thickened. Drizzle over strawberries and spinach. Serve immediately.

Salads & Dressings

71

Dried Fruit Salad

1	(10 oz) bag romaine lettuce hearts
1	(4 oz) pkg feta cheese, crumbled
½ C	pecan halves, toasted and salted
½	(6 oz) box croutons

Dressing

½ C	balsamic vinegar
½ C	olive oil
½ C	dried cherries
½ C	dried blueberries
1	red pear, thinly sliced

Combine all the ingredients for the dressing and let marinate for 1-2 hours. Add romaine, feta, pecans, and croutons to the marinating fruit and dressing. Toss and serve.

Salads & Dressings

Blue Cheese and Pear Salad with Port Vinaigrette

3	Bosc or red Bartlett pears, firm yet ripe
6	slices of bacon (optional)
2 C	ruby Port
1	shallot, sliced
1 C	olive oil
3 T	red wine vinegar
12 C	mixed baby greens
¾ C	blue cheese, crumbled

Cook bacon in heavy medium nonstick skillet over medium-high heat until crisp and brown, about 5 minutes. Transfer bacon to paper towels to drain. Coarsely chop bacon.

Bring Port and shallot to boil in a heavy medium saucepan; reduce heat to medium-low and simmer until reduced to ½ cup, about 10 minutes. Strain into large bowl; cool. Whisk oil and vinegar into port. Season with salt and pepper. Slice pears and toss gently with a small amount of dressing. Toss greens, cheese, and bacon with dressing. Divide among plates, garnish with pear slices, and serve.

Salads & Dressings

Mardi Gras Salad

1	head lettuce, shredded
1	(10 oz) bag spinach
1	small red onion, thinly sliced
10	slices bacon, fried and crumbled
2	small cans mandarin oranges, drained
1	(8 oz) package mushrooms, sliced

Dressing

⅔ C	oil
2 t	onions, chopped
½ C	cider vinegar
¼ C	sugar
1 t	salt
1 t	Dijon mustard

For the dressing put onion, cider, vinegar, sugar, salt, and mustard into blender. Start on low speed and slowly add oil. Blend well and refrigerate until ready to serve. Mix and toss all salad ingredients. Blend dressing again before serving. Pour over salad and toss well.

Salads & Dressings

The Ultimate Salad

SERVES
8-10

6 oz	spinach, rinsed and torn into bite-size pieces
½ C	dried cranberries
½ C	crumbled blue cheese
2	tomatoes, seeded and chopped
1	avocado, diced
¼	red onion, thinly sliced
¼-½ C	walnuts, chopped
2 T	red raspberry jam, seedless
2 T	red wine vinegar
⅓ C	walnut oil
	freshly ground pepper and salt

In a large bowl, toss together the spinach, cranberries, blue cheese, tomatoes, avocados, onion, and walnuts. Set aside in refrigerator. In a small bowl whisk together jam, vinegar, walnut oil, pepper, and salt. Taste and adjust amounts to suite your taste. Refrigerate until serving. Toss salad with enough dressing to coat spinach. Can add diced yellow and orange peppers.

INSIGHT: Walnut oil has a distinctive nutty flavor and fragrance. Although it is most often used in salad dressings, it may also be used for sautéing, in sauces and baked goods. It is best to store walnut oil in the refrigerator.

Salads & Dressings

Joyce's Salad and Dressing

¾ C	vegetable oil
¼ C	wine vinegar
½ t	Ac'cent
1 t	salt
1 t	sugar
1 t	dry mustard
1	clove garlic, finely minced
2 t	Worcestershire sauce
	toasted sesame seeds (optional)
	Romano cheese, grated
24 oz	lettuce greens

For dressing, mix all ingredients, oil through Worcestershire. Add toasted sesame seeds and grated Romano cheese to lettuce greens. Toss just before serving.

Caesar Salad with Southwestern Dressing

½ C	light mayonnaise
1½ T	chicken broth
1 T	soy sauce
1 T	fresh lemon juice
½ t	canned chipotle chilies, minced or pressed through a garlic press or ¼ t chipotle sauce
1	large head romaine lettuce, cut into bite-size pieces
2	medium tomatoes, seeded and diced
½ C	frozen corn kernels, thawed and drained
4 T	freshly grated Parmesan cheese

Whisk mayonnaise, chicken broth, soy sauce, lemon juice, and chipotles in a medium bowl to blend. Season dressing to taste with salt, pepper, and chipotle sauce. (Dressing can be prepared 1 day ahead. Cover and refrigerate.) Toss with remaining ingredients.

Salads & Dressings

Napa Cabbage Salad

Salad

1 lg	napa cabbage (or 2 small)
5-6	green onions, sliced thin including the dark green
2	(3 oz) pkg ramen noodles (do not use season packet)
½	stick butter, melted
¼ C	sesame seeds
4 oz	almonds, slivered

Dressing

½ C	pure vegetable oil
½ C	rice vinegar (in the Oriental section of market)
½ C	sugar
2½ t	light soy sauce

Thinly slice napa cabbage using a sharp knife as if you were slicing bread. Mix the cabbage and onion together. Melt butter in a large skillet. Sauté the almonds and sesame seeds until slightly brown then toss in crunched up ramen noodles. Mix well. Cool mixture and put in plastic container until ready to use.

Prepare the dressing by mixing all the ingredients together. Make the dressing the night before or 5 hours before and store in refrigerator. Shake well before adding to napa cabbage. Do not mix dressing with cabbage until ready to use.

Salads & Dressings

Broccoli Slaw Salad

Salad

1 lb	broccoli slaw
6	green onions, sliced
1	(3 oz) pkg chicken flavored ramen noodles
1 C	sunflower seeds

Dressing

⅓ C	oil
⅓ C	sugar
	chicken flavor pack from noodles
3 T	vinegar, red or white wine

Mix broccoli slaw, green onions, and broken-up noodles together, set aside.
Mix dressing ingredients together to dissolve sugar. Toss together 2 hours
before serving and refrigerate. Add sunflower seeds just before serving.
Season to taste.

Salads & Dressings

Barley Salad with Medley of Red Peppers, Corn and Portobellos

½ C	pearl barley, toasted
1½ C	vegetable or chicken broth
1	large poblano chili or green bell pepper
1	small red bell pepper
2	large plum tomatoes, about 1 C, seeded and chopped
1 C	fresh corn or frozen and thawed
⅓ C	fresh cilantro, chopped
¼ C	green onions, chopped
2½ T	fresh lime juice
2 T	olive oil
	nonstick olive oil spray
4	large portobello mushrooms, stemmed and dark gills scraped away
24	large spinach leaves

To toast barley, which gives it a nutty flavor, place barley in heavy large saucepan. Cook over medium heat until pale golden, shaking pan occasionally, about 10 minutes. Add broth to pan and bring to boil. Reduce heat to medium-low, cover and simmer until barley is tender and broth is absorbed, about 35 minutes. Uncover and let barley cool.

Char poblano and red bell pepper over gas flame or in broiler until blackened on all sides. Enclose in paper bag and let stand for 10 minutes. Peel, seed, and dice poblano and red bell pepper. Place barley, poblano, and red bell pepper in large bowl. Add tomatoes, corn, cilantro, onions, lime juice, and olive oil; toss to blend. Season salad with salt and pepper.

MAKE AHEAD: At this point, salad can be prepared and refrigerated for a day. Bring to room temperature before serving.

Prepare barbeque (medium-high heat). Spray mushrooms with nonstick spray; sprinkle with salt and pepper. Grill until cooked through, about 4 minutes per side. Transfer to work surface; slice thinly. Arrange 6 spinach leaves on each of the 4 plates. Top with barley salad. Arrange 1 sliced mushroom alongside each salad. Serve while mushrooms are still warm.

Salads & Dressings

Chipotle Corn Salad

SERVES
4-6

5	ears fresh corn, about 3 C kernels
2	roma tomatoes, seeded and chopped
3-4 T	fresh cilantro, minced
3 T	sweet onion, minced
3 T	olive oil
1 T	white wine vinegar
1	canned chipotle chile, seeded and minced (or pressed through a garlic press)
¾ t	adobo sauce from canned chipotles
2 t	fresh lime juice
¼ t	salt

Simmer corn 7 minutes. Remove the kernels from the ears of corn. Combine corn, tomatoes, cilantro, and onion. In a small jar shake together the remaining ingredients. Pour over corn. Serve at room temperature or chilled.

INSPIRATION: For additional flavor, roast the corn on a charcoal grill.

Salads & Dressings

Cucumber Vinaigrette Salad

3	cucumbers, peeled and halved lengthwise, seeded and thinly sliced (about 3½ cups)
½ C	red onion, thinly sliced
1 T	fresh basil, chopped or 1 t dried basil
1 T	fresh parsley, chopped or 1 t dried parsley
2 T	red wine vinegar
1 T	olive oil
2½ t	Dijon mustard
¼ t	salt

Place cucumbers and onion in a bowl. Combine basil and remaining ingredients, pour over cucumber mixture and toss gently. Cover and chill.

Roasted Asparagus Salad with Bell Peppers

2	medium red bell peppers, halved lengthwise
1	sweet onion, halved
¼ C	extra-virgin olive oil, plus more for brushing
2	garlic cloves, minced
	salt and freshly ground pepper
40	asparagus spears, trimmed and cut into 5" lengths
1 T	balsamic vinegar
¼ C	freshly grated Parmesan cheese

Preheat the oven to 400°. Brush the pepper skins and onion lightly with olive oil and set them, cut side down, on a baking sheet. Bake the peppers for 15 minutes or until the skins are blistered. (The peppers and onion can also be grilled.) Remove the skins, seeds, and cores and cut the pepper into long thin strips. Slice the onion into slivers. In a bowl, combine the roasted peppers and onion with ¼ cup of olive oil and the garlic; season with salt and pepper.

In a large pot of boiling salted water, cook asparagus until just tender, about 4 minutes, or microwave in small amount of water for 3-4 minutes. Drain the asparagus; refresh under cold running water. Pat the asparagus dry with paper towels.

MAKE AHEAD: Vegetables can be stored separately in the refrigerator overnight. Bring them to room temperature before proceeding.

Preheat the oven to 450°. Spread half of the roasted pepper and onions in the baking dish. Top with asparagus, season with salt and pepper. Top with the remaining roasted peppers and onions and spoon all the liquid on top. Bake for about 15 minutes, or until bubbling. Drizzle with the balsamic vinegar, Parmesan cheese, and serve warm.

Salads & Dressings

Red Potato with Green Bean Salad

4 oz	green beans, trimmed and cut into 1½" pieces
1½ lb	small red potatoes, unpeeled, cut into 1½" pieces
1 T	dry vermouth
1 T	white wine vinegar
⅓ C	light olive oil
2 T	shallots, chopped
1½ t	Dijon mustard
1 T	fresh parsley, chopped

Cook beans in saucepan of boiling salted water until crisp-tender, 4 minutes. Drain. Transfer to bowl of ice water. Drain; pat dry with paper towels. Cook potatoes in large pot of boiling salted water until just tender, about 12 minutes. Drain; transfer to a large bowl. Sprinkle vermouth over hot potatoes; toss gently and let stand for 5 minutes.

Whisk vinegar, shallots, and mustard in small bowl. Gradually whisk in oil. Blend well. Pour over potatoes and toss to coat. Cool completely. Mix in green beans and parsley. Season to taste with salt and pepper.

MAKE AHEAD: Can be made 1 day ahead, although green beans will discolor. Cover and refrigerate. Allow salad to come to room temperature before serving.

Salads & Dressings

84

Lime Potato Salad

2 lb	fingerlings or new baby potatoes, cut into ¾" dice with skin on
½ C	sweet onion, diced
1½ t	lime peel, grated
3 T	lime juice
1 T	light olive oil or vegetable oil
1 t	salt
1 C	cucumber, peeled, seeded, and chopped
1 C	yellow bell pepper, chopped
½ C	coleslaw-type dressing

Boil potatoes until tender, but don't let them get mushy. Drain well.
Meanwhile, mix onion, lime peel, lime juice, oil, and salt in a bowl large enough
to accommodate all the ingredients. Add warm potatoes and gently toss to
coat well. Cover and refrigerate for at least 1 hour. Gently stir in rest of
ingredients and refrigerate until chilled.

Salads & Dressings

Wild Rice Salad

Salad

⅔ C	uncooked wild rice, cooked
⅔ C	uncooked orzo, cooked
½	red bell pepper, chopped
½ C	kalamata olives, sliced
¼ C	sun-dried tomatoes, chopped
¼ C	pine nuts, toasted
¼ C	unsalted sunflower seeds
2 T	capers, drained and rinsed
½ C	green onions, chopped
2 T	fresh basil
¼ C	fresh Parmesan cheese, grated

Dressing

¼ C	olive oil
¼ C	balsamic vinegar
1	large garlic clove, crushed
¼ t	pepper

Shake together the dressing ingredients. For a less tart dressing substitute some of the balsamic with lemon juice.

Combine the remaining ingredients, rice through Parmesan. Toss with the dressing. Cover and chill at least 2 hours or overnight. Adjust seasoning before serving.

INSIGHT: To soften sun-dried tomatoes which are not oil-packed, cover with boiling water and let stand 2 minutes.

Salads & Dressings

Santa Fe Rice Salad

2 C	cooked white rice, chilled
¾ C	black beans or kidney beans, rinsed and drained
1	large tomato, seeded and diced
¾ C	sharp Cheddar cheese, diced
⅓ C	green onions, sliced
⅓ C	vegetable oil
¼ C	seasoned rice vinegar
1 T	canned chipotle chilies in adobo sauce or fresh jalapeño peppers, minced
¾ t	salt or to taste
½ t	sugar
1	small ripe avocado, diced

In a large bowl, combine rice, beans, tomato, cheese, and green onions; mix well. In a small bowl, combine remaining ingredients except avocado; mix well. Pour over rice mixture; mix well. Cover and refrigerate at least 30 minutes.

MAKE AHEAD: At this point, salad can be refrigerated up to 24 hours.

Just before serving check seasoning and gently stir in avocado. Serve chilled or at room temperature.

Salads & Dressings

Confetti Cornbread Salad

2	(6 oz) pkgs cornbread mix, baked and crumbled, (8 cups)
1	green pepper, chopped
1	red pepper, chopped
1 C	non-fat plain yogurt
1½ C	mayonnaise
3	stalks of celery, chopped
1 C	green onion, chopped
1 C	pecans, chopped
1 C	tomatoes, chopped and seeded

Mix all ingredients, adding the crumbled corn bread last and chill for 3 hours. This is best served the same day as prepared.

BLT Pasta Salad

8	slices of bacon, cooked crisp, and broken into ½" pieces
10	cherry tomatoes, halved
¾ C	Thousand Island dressing
¼ C	green onion, finely chopped
1	egg, hard-boiled and chopped
1 t	Worcestershire sauce
⅛ t	hot sauce
8 oz	spiral pasta
	leaf lettuce

Cook and drain pasta. Place bacon, tomatoes, green onions, and pasta in large mixing bowl. In another bowl combine dressing, onion, egg, Worcestershire, and hot sauce. Pour over pasta and combine. Refrigerate at least 1 hour.

Remove from refrigerator 30 minutes prior to serving. If salad appears dry, add a small amount of olive oil. To serve, arrange leaf lettuce on a platter spooning salad onto center.

INSPIRATION: One cup of diced cooked chicken is a nice addition.

Salads & Dressings

Winter Pasta Salad

Salad

12 oz	tri-color fusilli
1	red pepper, cut into matchsticks
1	yellow pepper, cut into matchsticks
½ pt	cherry tomatoes, halved or quartered
½ C	oil-packed sun-dried tomatoes, chopped and drained
⅓ lb	Genoa salami, cut into matchsticks
½ lb	pepperoni, cut into matchsticks
½ C	Parmesan cheese, grated
¼ C	fresh basil, shredded

Dressing

1 C	olive oil
⅓ C	balsamic vinegar
2 T	Dijon mustard
½ t	oregano
1-2 T	oil from the sun-dried tomatoes
	salt and pepper to taste

Cook pasta until al dente, rinse with cold water, and drain again. Thoroughly blend together the dressing ingredients, either by hand or in a blender or food processor. In a large bowl, toss together the salad ingredients and the dressing. Refrigerate at least 1 hour. Just before serving, toss again and adjust seasonings if necessary.

INSPIRATION: Add quartered artichoke hearts and diced pepperoncini.

Orzo and Spinach Salad

¾ lb	orzo (about 2 cups)
1 T	olive oil
½ C	olive oil
3 T	white wine vinegar
3 T	lemon juice
1 t	freshly ground pepper
1 t	Dijon mustard
1	small clove garlic, minced
pinch	thyme
½ t	dried oregano
¼ t	ground cumin
3 oz	spinach, washed and torn into bite-size pieces
1	red bell pepper, chopped
½ C	kalamata olives, pitted and slivered
½ C	scallions, minced
2 t	capers, rinsed and drained
3 T	feta cheese, crumbled
3 T	pine nuts, toasted

Cook orzo al dente. Rinse briefly in cold water and drain. Toss with 1 tablespoon olive oil. Prepare dressing by combining remaining oil through cumin, whisking until smooth. Toss with orzo. Add spinach, pepper, olives, scallions, and capers. At this point, salad can be refrigerated several hours. At serving time, add crumbled feta cheese and pine nuts.

Salads & Dressings

Thai Beef Salad

1½ lbs	beef tenderloin, at room temperature
¼ C	fresh cilantro, coarsely chopped
2 T	fresh mint, coarsely chopped
1	large jalapeño pepper, minced
3	large garlic cloves, crushed through a press
2 T	Asian fish sauce
2 T	light brown sugar
¼ C	fresh lime juice
1	head of lettuce, leaves separated
2	tomatoes, thinly sliced
1	small cucumber, thinly sliced
1	small red onion, thinly sliced
	freshly ground black pepper
1	lime, cut into thin wedges

Preheat the oven to 500°. Set the beef tenderloin in a small baking dish and roast for 20 minutes, until rare. Let cool for 30 minutes, then refrigerate until cool, about 2 hours.

Slice the tenderloin against the grain into ¼-inch-thick slices. Then cut into strips about ¼-inch wide. In a large bowl, combine the meat strips, cilantro, mint, and jalapeño pepper; and toss. In a small bowl, combine the garlic, fish sauce, brown sugar, and lime juice; mix well. Pour this dressing over the meat and toss to coat.

Cover a large plate or platter with lettuce leaves. Arrange the tomatoes around the outside, overlapping the slices as necessary. Arrange the cucumber slices inside the tomatoes and then the onion slices inside those. Remove the meat from the dressing and mound it in the center of the vegetables. Pour any dressing that remains in the bowl over the meat. Cover the salad with a damp towel and refrigerate until chilled, at least 1 hour and up to 4 hours. Before serving, sprinkle with black pepper and garnish with the lime wedges.

INSPIRATION: Use leftover roasted beef tenderloin to prepare this salad.

Salads & Dressings

Craig's Favorite Chicken Curry Salad

2 C	chicken stock
1 lb	chicken breasts, boneless and skinless
¼ C	slivered almonds
½ C	mayonnaise
3 T	heavy whipping cream
½ t	curry powder
pinch	sugar
⅔ C	red and green grapes, mixed, and cut in half

Bring the chicken stock to a boil in large saucepan and add the chicken breasts. Let the stock come back to a simmer, lower the heat, and cook gently for 20-25 minutes, partially covered. Lift the breasts out of the stock and cool.

Scatter the almonds on a baking sheet and lightly toast for 6-8 minutes in an oven heated to 325°. Thoroughly blend the mayonnaise, whipping cream, and curry powder and season to taste with sugar.

To assemble, cut the cooled chicken breasts into large chunks. Place the chicken, almonds, and grapes in a mixing bowl. Add as much of the dressing as necessary to reach a consistency you like.

Salads & Dressings

Rotisserie Chicken Salads

Rosemary Chicken Salad

1	rotisserie chicken
½ C	mayonnaise
2 T	fresh rosemary, minced
	salt and pepper to taste

Pull chicken from bones and shred or dice as desired. Stir in mayonnaise, starting with ½ cup. Add more mayonnaise as desired Add rosemary and mix thoroughly. Add salt and pepper to taste. Chicken salad is better if allowed to sit covered in refrigerator for a few hours.

Crunchy Ginger Chicken Salad

1	rotisserie chicken
¼ C	sour cream
¼ C	mayonnaise
½ C	celery, finely diced
2 T	crystallized ginger, minced
	salt to taste

Pull chicken from bones and finely dice chicken. Stir sour cream and mayonnaise into diced chicken until all chicken has been moistened. Add more mayonnaise if needed. Stir in celery and ginger. Add salt to taste. Cover salad and chill for 2-3 hours before serving.

INSPIRATION: An easy way to mince crystallized ginger is to place ginger in the freezer for an hour or 2 before mincing.

Salads & Dressings

Rotisserie Chicken Salads
(Continued)

Sun-Dried Tomato Basil Chicken Salad

1	rotisserie chicken
½ C	mayonnaise
⅓ C	sun-dried tomatoes packed in oil, chopped and drained
2 t	oil from sun-dried tomatoes
1 t	fresh basil, minced
	salt and pepper to taste

Pull chicken from bone. Cut chicken into ½-inch dice. Stir mayonnaise and tomatoes into chicken. Stir in oil and more mayonnaise if needed. Add fresh basil and salt and pepper to taste. Refrigerate for 3-4 hours before serving.

INSPIRATION: Rotisserie chickens make creative chicken salads so easy! If you only want to use the white meat in these salads, freeze the dark meat with the rest of the carcass to make our Rotisserie Chicken Stock (see Index) at a later date. Don't be afraid to combine 2 or 3 different ingredients to create your own salad ideas. Consider adding pesto, and grated parmesan, or chopped shallots and fresh tarragon.

Salads & Dressings

Roasted Chicken Salad

¼ lb	pancetta, paper thin
1	rotisserie chicken, cut into 1" pieces
1 C	carrots, grated
1 C	celery, sliced
¾ C	green beans, blanched and refreshed – cut into 1" pieces
½ C	radish, grated
2 T	jalapeños, seeded and minced (or to taste)
½ C	mayonnaise
1 T	lemon juice
⅛ t	cayenne
1 t	kosher salt
	fresh pepper
2 C	arugula or spinach leaves, cleaned
2	medium tomatoes, cored and sliced ½" thick

Preheat oven to 375°. Put pancetta on baking sheet and bake until crisp, about 20 minutes. Pat pancetta with a paper towel.

Combine chicken with carrots, celery, green beans, radish, jalapeños, mayonnaise, lemon juice, cayenne, and salt. Arrange arugula or spinach to cover platter. Spoon salad onto center with tomato slices around chicken salad and top with crisped pancetta.

Salads & Dressings

French Chicken Salad

2 C	fresh green beans (½ lb)
4 C	stock or water, seasoned with salt, pepper, onion, and celery
2	boneless, skinless chicken breasts (about ¾ lb)
4 C	baby greens
⅓ C	raspberry vinaigrette (your favorite or see Index)
½ pt	fresh raspberries
	Parmesan (or blue) cheese, grated
	salt
	freshly cracked pepper
¼ C	sweet onion, very thinly sliced (optional)

Blanch beans in water or stock for 4-6 minutes or until just tender. Set aside and while chicken is poaching, trim ends diagonally and cut beans in 2-inch diagonal pieces. Poach (slow simmer) chicken in water or stock for 8-10 minutes or until barely pink inside. Put in refrigerator, if not serving within 30 minutes. Bring to room temperature or warm briefly in microwave before serving.

Wash and dry greens. Put in large salad bowl, adding optional onion. Toss greens with 2 tablespoons vinaigrette. Toss beans with 1 tablespoon vinaigrette and arrange over greens. Thinly slice chicken and arrange over beans. Sprinkle raspberries over salad. Pour remaining dressing over all. Season with cheese, salt, and pepper.

INSPIRATION: A delicious lady's luncheon salad.

Salads & Dressings

Shades of Brown Rice Salad

Salad

2 C	cooked chicken, cut into bite-sized pieces
2⅓ C	boiling water
1½ t	ginger, ground
1 t	salt
1 C	brown rice
½ C	celery, sliced thin
½ C	dates, chopped
½ C	walnuts, coarsely chopped
½ t	orange zest or more to taste
2	oranges cut up

Dressing

½ C	sour cream
½ C	mayonnaise
1 T	lemon juice
2 t	sugar

Add ginger, salt, and rice to boiling water. Cover and simmer until water is absorbed and rice is tender. While rice is cooking prepare the rest of the salad ingredients in a large bowl. Mix the dressing ingredients. Let rice cool to just warm before adding to bowl. Toss with the dressing. Serve on lettuce leaves.

INSPIRATION: In place of the dates, use dried cranberries or cherries.

Salads & Dressings

Seafood Pasta Salad

1½ lb	mussels, scrubbed
1½ lb	small clams, scrubbed
½ C	dry white wine or water
10 oz	fettuccine
¼ C	olive oil
3 T	fresh lemon juice
1	clove garlic, minced
	salt and pepper
¼ C	fresh basil leaves
2 T	fresh parsley

Heat wine in a pot and bring to a boil, add clams, and simmer 5 minutes or until shells open. Remove clams. Repeat with mussels. Discard liquid. Cool seafood and remove from shells. Set aside.

Cook pasta and drain. Combine pasta, oil, lemon juice, garlic, salt, pepper, and seafood, marinate 20 minutes.

Chop basil and parsley and add to pasta. Toss gently. Serve at room temperature.

Salads & Dressings

99

White Bean and Tuna Salad

2	(16 oz) cans cannelloni beans, drained and rinsed
2	(7 oz) cans tuna packed in olive oil, drained and flaked
1	small red onion, chopped
1 C	Italian parsley, chopped
1	red bell pepper, chopped
½ C	cured, pitted black olives, sliced
1 C	celery, diced (optional for crunch)
	juice and zest of 2 lemons, or more to taste
½ C	olive oil
½-¾ C	pepperoncini, chopped
	salt and freshly ground black pepper to taste
	fresh greens for garnish

Combine all the ingredients, except beans and tuna, in a large bowl. Fold in beans and tuna gently to combine. Allow to rest in refrigerator for several hours or overnight to allow flavors to develop. Season to taste and serve on a platter lined with fresh greens.

Salads & Dressings

Rosy Shrimp Salad

1	small pkg lemon gelatin
1	(10 oz) can tomato soup
8 oz	cream cheese
1 C	mayonnaise
1 t	Worcestershire sauce
½ t	hot sauce
¼ t	salt
½ C	celery, chopped
½ C	green pepper, chopped
½ C	sweet onion, minced
1 lb	cooked shrimp (cut if large)

Dissolve gelatin in ⅓ cup hot water. Melt cream cheese with soup and heat thoroughly (a double boiler is handy for this.) Add gelatin mixture and heat again. Cool slightly and add mayonnaise, Worcestershire sauce, hot sauce, and salt. Mix well. Cool before adding remaining ingredients. Pour into an 8 x 8-inch pan or loaf pan. Refrigerate until molded. Use a sharp knife to cut. May be garnished with mayonnaise flavored with a pinch of curry.

INSPIRATION: This salad is perfect for a ladies luncheon served as part of a trio with chicken salad and fruit salad.

Salads & Dressings

101

Blue Cheese Dressing

8 oz	blue cheese, a high quality creamy variety
2 T	vinegar
2 C	sour cream
1½ t	garlic salt, use more to taste
½ t	celery salt
1½ t	Hungarian paprika, use more to taste
½ t	black pepper
½ C	mayonnaise

Mix ingredients together and refrigerate overnight.

Makes 3 cups.

Poppy Seed Dressing

1 C	sugar
2 t	dry mustard
2 t	salt
⅔ C	vinegar
3 T	onion juice
3 T	poppy seeds
2 C	salad oil

Add all ingredients and shake in a jar. Best if NOT done in a blender.

Makes 3½ cups.

Raspberry Vinaigrette

¼ C	raspberry vinegar
½ C	light olive oil
¾ t	Dijon
¼ t	salt
¼ t	sugar
	freshly ground pepper

Combine all ingredients in a jar and shake well. Delicious tossed with a green salad, dried cherries or cranberries, goat or blue cheese, red onion, and toasted nuts.

Makes ¾ cup.

Edna's Dressing

2 C	light or regular mayonnaise
1	large dill pickle
½	medium onion, grated
¼ C	catsup
1 t	Worcestershire sauce
¼	seasoned salt

Place all ingredients into blender and process until smooth. Chill. Serve as a dressing or dip.

Makes 2½ cups.

INSPIRATION: Very good as a dip for steamed artichokes.

Lemony French Salad Dressing

½ C	olive oil
1-2	cloves garlic, minced
2 T	white wine vinegar
2 T	fresh lemon juice
1 t	salt
½ t	freshly ground black pepper

Combine all ingredients in a bottle and shake vigorously. Chill in refrigerator several hours or overnight.

Makes ¾ cup.

Healthy Sun-Dried Tomato Dressing

½ C	sun-dried tomatoes (not oil-packed)
½ C	water
2 t	oil
½ C	chicken broth, undiluted
3 T	red wine vinegar
2 T	Dijon mustard
2	shallots
1	clove garlic, crushed
¼ t	salt
⅛ t	pepper

Combine tomatoes, water, and oil; let stand for 1 hour. Finely chop in food processor, including liquid. Add remaining ingredients and process until smooth. Serve on greens or toss with cold pasta. This is a low calorie dressing with 9 calories per tablespoon.

Makes 1½ cups.

Dressings

Pistachio-Lime Vinaigrette Salad Dressing

⅓ C	fresh lime juice
2-3 T	honey
3 T	purple onions, chopped
½ t	dried crushed red pepper
¼ t	salt
3 T	fresh parsley, chopped
⅔ C	vegetable oil
½ C	pistachios (2 oz)
1-3 T	water

Process lime juice, honey, onions, red pepper, salt, and parsley in food processor until smooth. With processor running, add oil in a slow, steady stream. Turn off; add pistachios, and pulse until pistachios are finely chopped. Store dressing in refrigerator.

Dressing will be thick so before serving, add water to thin to desired consistency, adjust seasoning to taste. To serve dressing, toss with spinach and fresh fruit, or mixed greens.

Makes about 2 cups.

INSPIRATION: Use dressing (before thinning with water) as a dip with fresh vegetables, shrimp or chicken fingers.

MAIN

Trout Amandine

2 lbs	sole, flounder, trout, or tilapia fillets – ½" thick
¼ C	flour
1 t	seasoned salt
1 t	paprika
¼ C	butter, melted
½ C	almonds, sliced
2 T	lemon juice
⅛ t	hot sauce
1 T	parsley, chopped

Preheat oven to broil. Cut fillets into 6 portions. Combine flour, seasoned salt, and paprika. Roll portions in flour mixture and place in a single layer, skin-side down, in a well greased shallow baking dish or broiling pan. Drizzle 2 tablespoons melted butter over portions.

Broil about 4-inches (place the oven rack in upper third of oven) from source of heat for 8 minutes for sole, trout, and flounder, 10 minutes for tilapia, or until fish flakes easily when tested with a fork.

While fish is broiling, sauté almonds in remaining butter until golden brown, stirring constantly. Remove from heat and mix in lemon juice, hot sauce, and parsley. Pour over portions and serve at once.

Seafood

Red Snapper Veracruz

6	(6 oz) red snapper or other firm white fish fillets
¼ C	fresh lime juice
1 T	olive oil
1½ C	onion, thinly sliced
4	garlic cloves, minced
3 lbs	ripe tomatoes, seeded and chopped (or canned plum tomatoes)
1 C	small green olives, sliced and divided
½ C	water
¼ C	capers, divided
¼ C	pickled jalapeño or poblano peppers, divided and sliced
1½ t	oregano
3	bay leaves
1 t	salt, divided
	flat-leaf parsley sprigs (optional)

Preheat oven to 350°. Arrange fish in single layer in a 13 x 9-inch baking dish, drizzle with lime juice, and sprinkle with ½ teaspoon salt. Cover and marinate in refrigerator for 30 minutes, discard marinade.

Heat the olive oil in a Dutch oven over medium-high heat. Add onion and garlic, and sauté for 5 minutes or until lightly browned. Add tomatoes, ½ cup olives, water, 2 tablespoons capers, 2 tablespoons peppers, oregano, and bay leaves. Bring to a boil, reduce heat and simmer 15-20 minutes to reduce excess liquid. Stir in ½ teaspoon salt. Discard bay leaves.

Spoon half of sauce over fish. Bake for 15 minutes or until fish flakes easily when tested with a fork. To serve, top with remaining sauce, olives, capers, and peppers. Garnish with parsley sprigs, if desired.

Seafood

Roasted Fish

4	**(5-6 oz) pieces of salmon, halibut, grouper, or red snapper, about 1½" thick**
¼ C	**butter, melted**
½-¾ C	**Panko breadcrumbs (or very fine white breadcrumbs)**
	salt and pepper

Preheat the oven to 400°. Line baking dish with foil and spray with oil. Add fillets, skin-side down. Drizzle or brush fillets with butter. Sprinkle bread crumbs over tops and season well with salt and pepper. Roast fish until opaque or flakes, 15-20 minutes. Serve with our Tomato, Cucumber, and Caper Relish (see Index).

Seafood

Salmon Bake with Pecans

4	(4-6 oz) salmon fillets
⅛ t	salt
⅛ t	pepper
2 T	Dijon mustard
2 T	butter, melted
1½ T	honey
¼ C	soft breadcrumbs
¼ C	pecans, finely chopped
2 t	fresh parsley, chopped
	fresh parsley sprigs, lemon slices (garnish)

Sprinkle salmon with salt and pepper. Place fillets, skin side down, in a lightly greased 13 x 9 x 2-inch pan. Combine mustard, butter, and honey. Brush mixture on the fillets. Combine breadcrumbs, pecans, and chopped parsley; spoon mixture evenly on top of each fillet. Bake at 450° for 10 minutes or until fish flakes easily with fork. Garnish.

Seafood

Smoked Salmon in a Bag

SERVES
4-6

1½-2 lb	salmon fillet
1 C	soy sauce
¾ C	brown sugar
½ C	water
¼ C	dry sherry
1"	piece of ginger, grated
1 T	garlic, chopped
2 t	kosher salt
1	Williams Seafood Smoker bag

Mix soy sauce, brown sugar, water, sherry, ginger, garlic, and salt together until sugar dissolves. Place salmon in glass pan and pour marinade over it. Marinate in refrigerator 4-24 hours.

Preheat oven to 450°. Place salmon in smoker bag and smoke in oven 25-30 minutes. Remove from oven and let rest in bag for 10 minutes. Serve hot or refrigerate and serve as a cold dish.

INSPIRATION: The smoker bags can be purchased by the meat and seafood counters. Try the other varieties of bags with chicken and meat.

seafood

Poached Salmon
Warm or Chilled

2 lb	center cut salmon fillet, skin removed, or 4 (6-8 oz) pieces
3 C	water
1¼ C	vermouth
¼	onion, sliced
6	peppercorns
1 T	salt

Combine water, vermouth, onion, and peppercorns. Bring to a simmer, add salt and reduce heat to low. Add salmon and poach until cooked through, about 9 minutes per inch of thickness. Remove from liquid and serve warm.

For chilled salmon, allow salmon to cool while still in liquid and then refrigerate. Remove from liquid when ready to serve.

Serve with either Soy Ginger Sauce or Cucumber Yogurt Sauce. (see next page)

Seafood

Soy-Ginger Sauce

1 T	fresh ginger, grated or finely minced
1 T	salad oil
1 T	sesame oil
2 T	soy sauce
6 T	lime juice
3 T	fresh basil, chopped (optional)

Whisk together thoroughly. Drizzle over the fish before serving.

Cucumber Yogurt Sauce

½ C	yogurt (non-fat plain)
½ C	sour cream
¼ C	green onion, minced
¼ C	cilantro, chopped
¼ t	cumin
¼ C	cucumber, peeled, seeded, and diced
⅛ t	salt

Mix thoroughly.

Fresh Salmon Cakes

1	(4-6 oz) salmon steak, cooked
2 T	green onions, chopped
1 T	mayonnaise
2 t	dry breadcrumbs
2 t	lemon juice
½	egg, beaten
¼ t	oregano, crushed
¼ t	cracked black pepper
2 T	flour
1 T	cornmeal
½ t	Dijon mustard
1 T	cilantro
2 t	red bell pepper
	butter
	vegetable oil

Flake salmon in a bowl. Add green onions, mayonnaise, breadcrumbs, lemon juice, egg, and seasonings. Blend thoroughly. Cover and refrigerate at least 30 minutes. Shape into 4 cakes. Mixture will be very moist and soft.

Combine flour and cornmeal and coat each side of the cakes. Melt 1 tablespoon each butter and oil in a 10" skillet. Panfry over medium to medium-high heat for 3-4 minutes per side or until golden.

INSPIRATION: The next time you grill salmon, plan on having leftovers to prepare these salmon cakes.

Seafood

Roasted Salmon with Cilantro Pesto

2 lbs	salmon fillets or 4 (6-8 oz) portions
1	garlic clove
1 C	cilantro leaves, loosely packed
2 T	olive oil
2 T	lime juice
	salt and freshly ground pepper
2-3	ripe roma tomatoes, seeded and chopped

Preheat the oven to 400°. Make the pesto in a food processor or blender; process the garlic, cilantro, oil, and lime juice until creamy. Season to taste.

Spray baking pan with oil and place the salmon skin-side down. Spread the pesto on the salmon, cover with the chopped tomatoes and season with salt and pepper. Bake uncovered for 15-18 minutes.

Seafood

Baked Haddock or Halibut

1-1¼ lb	**haddock or halibut**
⅓ C	**reduced fat sour cream**
1 t	**Dijon mustard**
¼ C	**Parmesan cheese, grated**
	paprika
	lemon or lime wedges
	salt and pepper

Preheat oven to 450°. Put fish onto lightly oiled broiling pan. Sprinkle with salt and pepper. Stir together sour cream, mustard, and Parmesan cheese. Spread over fish and sprinkle with paprika. Place on middle oven rack and bake 12 minutes per inch of thickness or until cooked through. Serve with lemon or lime wedges.

Seafood

Halibut with Wild Mushrooms

4	(6 oz) halibut fillets with skin, about 1½" thick
2 T	olive oil
2 lbs	assorted mushrooms (white, shiitake, oyster, or chanterelle; stems trimmed or discarded, large mushrooms cut into quarters)
5 T	cold unsalted butter, 2 T cut into pieces
	salt and freshly ground pepper
3	medium leeks, washed well, white and tender green parts finely chopped
½ C	chicken stock
2 T	vegetable oil
¼ C	fresh flat-leaf parsley, finely chopped

Heat the olive oil in a large skillet until almost smoking. Add the mushrooms and cook over moderately high heat, stirring for 2 minutes. Stir in 1 tablespoon of the butter, reduce the heat to low and cook until the mushrooms are browned and the pan is dry, about 7 minutes. Season with salt and pepper and transfer to a saucepan.

Melt 2 more tablespoons of butter in the skillet. Add the leeks, cover and cook over low heat stirring a few times until tender, about 10 minutes. Season with salt and pepper. Add to the mushrooms along with the chicken stock; simmer for 3 minutes. Season with salt and pepper. Keep warm.

Preheat the oven to 450°. In a heavy-bottomed ovenproof skillet, heat the vegetable oil until almost smoking. Season the fish with salt and pepper and add to the skillet, skin-side down. Shake the skillet to loosen the fillets and cook over high heat until the skin is browned and crisp, about 5 minutes. Turn the fillets, transfer the skillet to the oven and roast for about 4 minutes, or until the fish is just cooked through.

Stir the butter pieces and chopped parsley into the mushroom-leek sauce. As soon as butter melts, divide the vegetable sauce among 4 large plates and set the fillets on top. Serve at once.

Seafood

121

Any Day Grilled Fish

1-1½ lbs   fish fillet or steaks; a firm fish is preferred, such
            as grouper, swordfish, or halibut

Lemon-Soy Marinade
2 T   soy sauce
¼ t   garlic powder or 1 clove, minced
¼ t   hot sauce
¼ C   fresh lemon juice
¼ t   pepper
2 T   olive oil

Combine ingredients for marinade in a jar and shake until well blended. Place fish in a shallow dish and cover with marinade. Marinate fish in refrigerator for up to 1 hour. Grill fish over medium heat (300°-400°) for about 6 minutes per side depending on thickness of fish.

INSPIRATION: Excellent served with our Confetti Pepper Relish (see Index).

Seafood

Grouper With Golden Tomato Caper Sauce

SERVES
4-6

2 lbs	grouper fillets
1	(1 oz pkg) hollandaise sauce
2 T	lemon juice
4 T	green onion, sliced thin
¾ C	seeded tomatoes, finely chopped
3 T	capers, rinsed and drained
½ t	sugar
¾ C	dry white wine or vermouth
2 T	butter
1 T	olive oil
	salt and pepper to taste

Prepare hollandaise mix according to directions. Once hollandaise sauce is completed, add lemon juice, green onion, tomatoes, capers and sugar. Stir gently to mix all ingredients. Add white wine and gently stir for 10 minutes on low heat or until wine and hollandaise have mellowed. Add butter and continue to stir until butter has melted into the sauce. Cover sauce and keep warm.

Preheat broiler. Arrange grouper fillets on broiler pan. Brush fillets with olive oil. Season with salt and pepper to taste. Broil fish 4 inches from heat, about 10 minutes, or until fish flakes easily with a fork.

Serve fish at once with sauce spooned over top.

Seafood

Marinated Orange Roughy

1 lb	orange roughy

Marinade

½ C	orange juice
¼ C	ketchup
2 T	soy sauce
2 T	brown sugar
dash	salt and pepper

Combine ingredients for marinade. Marinate fish for 30 minutes in refrigerator. Grill. Fish is done when it flakes easily.

Fish Tacos with Tomatillo Sauce

Fish

1½ lb	mahi-mahi fillets
3 T	lime or lemon juice
1	garlic clove, crushed
1 T	oil
1 t	cumin, ground
8	8" flour or corn tortillas

Sauce

1 lb	tomatillos, husked, rinsed, and quartered
¼ C	chicken stock
2	cloves garlic
½ C	onion
2	serrano or jalapeño peppers, halved and seeded (optional)
½ t	sugar
1 T	lime or lemon juice
	salt and pepper to taste
½ C	cilantro leaves, chopped

Combine lemon or lime juice, garlic clove, oil and cumin. Marinate fish in juice mixture 30-45 minutes. Preheat the grill and grill fish about 4 minutes per side basting with marinade.

Meanwhile prepare sauce. Begin by simmering tomatillos for 5 minutes in stock. Process garlic, onion, and peppers until chopped. Add cooked tomatillos, sugar, and lime and process until coarsely pureed. Season with salt and pepper. Flavor will be somewhat tart. Add more stock for a thinner stock. Reheat before serving, adding cilantro just before serving.

MAKE AHEAD: This sauce can be made up to a day ahead.

As the fish grills, prepare the tortillas for heating by layering tortillas between wax paper or slightly dampened paper towels. Place the stack of tortillas in a casserole with a tight fitting lid. When ready to serve, place casserole dish in the microwave for about 1 minute. Timing will depend on size of tortillas and power of microwave.

To serve tacos, place a piece of the grilled fish in a warm tortilla and top with the tomatillo sauce.

INSPIRATION: Tomatillo sauce is also great served with chicken and pork!

Seafood

125

Tuna with White Beans and Sun-dried Tomatoes

1 C	dried Great Northern beans (about 6½ oz)
5 C	chicken broth
4 T	olive oil
½ C	onion, chopped
½ C	carrot, chopped
½ C	celery, chopped
1 T	fresh thyme, chopped or 1 tsp dried thyme
1 T	lemon peel, grated
4	(6-8 oz) sushi-grade tuna steaks, each ¾-1" thick
	Sun-dried Tomato Sauce (see next page)

Place beans in medium bowl. Add enough cold water to cover beans by 3 inches. Let stand overnight. Drain. Combine beans and stock in large saucepan. Bring to boil. Reduce heat to medium; cover and simmer until beans are just tender, about 1 hour. Drain, reserving ½ cup cooking liquid.

Heat 2 tablespoons of oil in heavy large skillet over medium heat. Add onion, carrots, and celery and sauté until almost tender, about 5 minutes. Add thyme and lemon peel and stir for 1 minute. Add beans and reserved ½ cup cooking liquid. Toss until heated through, about 5 minutes. Season to taste with salt and pepper. Remove from heat and cover to keep warm.

Heat remaining 2 tablespoons of oil in another heavy large skillet over medium-high heat. Sprinkle tuna with salt and pepper. Add tuna to skillet and cook to desired doneness, about 3 minutes per side for medium. Tuna can also be grilled.

Spoon beans onto center of each of 4 plates, dividing equally among plates. Top each with tuna steak. Spoon Sun-dried Tomato Sauce over the tuna steaks and serve immediately.

INSPIRATION: To save time, you can substitute canned cannellini beans for dried beans. Rinse and drain the beans and add to sautéed vegetables along with ½ cup chicken broth.

Seafood

Sun-dried Tomato Sauce

½ C	oil-packed sun-dried tomatoes, drained
1 C	dry white wine
¼ C	white wine vinegar
10	black peppercorns
1 C	whipping cream
½ C	chicken broth
2 t	fresh thyme, minced or ½ tsp dried

Place sun-dried tomatoes in food processor. Boil white wine, white wine vinegar, and black peppercorns in heavy small saucepan until liquid is reduced to 3 tablespoons, about 8 minutes. Strain liquid into tomatoes in processor and purée until smooth. Return tomato mixture to same saucepan. Add whipping cream, chicken stock, and thyme. Simmer until flavors blend, about 3 minutes. Season to taste with salt.

Makes about 1½ cups.

INSPIRATION: In place of the sun-dried tomato sauce, use a red bell pepper sauce. In either case, a purchased jar of tapenade is an easy alternative.

Seafood

Seared Tuna Encrusted with Sesame Seeds

8 oz	1" sushi-grade tuna fillet
2 T	black or white sesame seeds, or a combination of both
	vegetable oil

Wash and dry tuna fillet. Cover both sides heavily with sesame seeds. Heat cast iron or other heavy skillet to hot (a few drops of water will sizzle). Coat skillet with just enough oil to cover. Cook tuna 2 minutes per side for rare and 3 minutes per side for medium-rare. This preparation of tuna is best served rare or medium-rare.

Serve whole or slice thinly across the grain. Garnish with chopped scallions and offer teriyaki sauce.

INSPIRATION: As a first course, serve several slices along with our Cucumber Vinaigrette (see Index).

Seafood

Barbequed Shrimp

5 lbs	fresh large shrimp (unpeeled)
1	bunch celery with leaves, coarsely chopped
3-4	garlic cloves, chopped
6	lemons, cut in halves
1 lb	butter, cut into cubes
1-2 oz	cracked black pepper
	Worcestershire sauce to taste
1-2 T	salt
	hot sauce to taste
	crusty bread

Preheat broiler. Wash shrimp and place in very large shallow pan. Add celery and garlic. Squeeze lemons over top and reserve squeezed lemon halves. Dot shrimp with butter and sprinkle with remaining seasonings. Arrange lemon halves on top. Place shrimp under broiler until butter melts and shrimp starts to turn pink (about 5 minutes), stirring several times. When all shrimp are slightly pink, reduce heat to bake at 350° and cook 20-30 minutes or until done, stirring often. *Do not overbake.* Taste for doneness. Serve hot with juices. Serve with plenty of crusty hot bread to dip in juices and extra napkins!

MAKE AHEAD: The flavor improves when prepared a day ahead. Make certain not to overcook shrimp; cool, cover, and refrigerate. When ready to serve, allow shrimp to sit at room temperature for 30 minutes before reheating in a preheated 350° oven. Heat, covered, just long enough to warm shrimp, 10-15 minutes.

Seafood

Shrimp Scampi

2 lbs	large shrimp
2 T	olive oil
2	garlic cloves, minced
¼ C	green onions, chopped
¼ C	white wine or vermouth
2 T	parsley, minced
1 t	salt
¼ t	pepper

Peel and devein the shrimp. Heat the olive oil in a sauté pan medium to medium-high. Add the garlic (do not brown), green onions and sauté 1 minute. Add the shrimp and sauté just until they turn pink. Add the wine and cook until it begins to simmer. Sprinkle with parsley and stir in the salt and pepper. Serve with rice or pasta.

Seafood

Greek-Style Scampi

1 t	olive oil
3-4	garlic cloves, minced
½ C	fresh parsley, chopped
2 t	dry oregano
1	(14 oz) can plum tomatoes, drained and coarsely chopped
¼ t	freshly ground black pepper
8-12 oz	chicken broth
1¼ lb	large shrimp, peeled and deveined
8 oz	angel hair pasta
¼ C	kalamata olives, chopped
2-3 C	baby spinach
1 C	crumbled feta cheese
2 T	fresh lemon juice

Heat oil in a large saucepan over medium heat. Add garlic, sauté 30 seconds. Add ¼ cup parsley, oregano, tomatoes, pepper, and chicken broth. Reduce heat, and simmer 10 minutes, season to taste. Add shrimp and cook for 3 minutes. Add spinach and olives and stir, and continue to cook 2-3 minutes.

Meanwhile, cook pasta until al dente. Just before serving add lemon juice and feta cheese. Serve over pasta. Garnish with remaining parsley.

seafood

Shrimp Stuffed with Crab Meat

1½ lb	large shrimp – shelled, deveined, and split open
1 lb	backfin or lump crab, picked for shell
¼ C	mayonnaise
1	egg, beaten lightly
1 t	white wine Worcestershire
1 T	parsley, chopped
1 T	chives, chopped
	zest of one lemon
¼ C	butter
1¼ C	fresh breadcrumbs
	parsley, chopped (optional)

Preheat oven to 375°.   Lay shrimp in a greased 9 x 13-inch pan in one layer to cover bottom of pan and refrigerate while making crab stuffing.
Mix mayonnaise, egg, Worcestershire, lemon zest, parsley, and chives. Season with salt and pepper if desired. Fold in crab meat. Top shrimp with crab.

Melt butter in sauté pan and lightly toast breadcrumbs. Sprinkle over stuffed shrimp. Sprinkle with chopped parsley if desired.

MAKE AHEAD: At this point, shrimp can be refrigerated up to 6 hours.

Cover loosely with foil and bake in oven until shrimp in center of casserole is no longer opaque, about 15 minutes. Serve immediately.

INSPIRATION: This is a wonderful recipe to serve as an entrée, and any leftovers can be added to cooked pasta with about 1 cup of the pasta water. Heat lightly covered until the shrimp are warmed through. Toss pasta and shrimp with lemon juice, olive oil and Parmesan to taste.

Seafood

Brined and Grilled Shrimp

1 qt	water
⅓ C	salt
⅓ C	light brown sugar (packed)
1½ lb	uncooked large shrimp, unpeeled
¼ C	olive oil
2 T	dry white wine
2	garlic cloves, minced
1 T	fresh parsley, chopped
¼ t	chipotle sauce

Stir water, salt, and brown sugar in medium bowl until sugar dissolves. Add shrimp. Refrigerate for at least 1 hour and up to 3 hours. Drain and rinse shrimp. (If brining peeled shrimp, brine only 30 minutes, drain and rinse.)

Using shears, cut shrimp shells down center of the back all the way to tail section. Using a sharp knife, cut shrimp in their shells along the full length of the back (do not cut all the way through). Remove vein and pull off legs. Open shrimp.

Whisk olive oil, white wine, garlic, parsley, and chipotle sauce in a medium bowl. Add shrimp and stir; let stand for 30 minutes. Prepare barbeque to medium-high heat. Place shrimp, flesh-side down, on grill. Grill shrimp until pink and cooked through.

INSPIRATION: You can also peel shrimp before marinating and grilling. Grill open face down in a foil pan. This shrimp is delicious served with our Creamy Stone-Ground Grits (see Index).

INSIGHT: Brining the shrimp and then grilling them in their shells will help retain flavor and the natural juices.

Seafood

Shrimp and Artichokes in Herbed Butter Sauce

1	(14 oz) can artichoke hearts
½	red bell pepper, roasted and sliced thin
1	¼" thick prosciutto slice, cut into thin slivers
½ C	chicken broth
1	large garlic clove
1 T	fresh lemon juice or to taste
1 t	freshly ground pepper
2 t	Worcestershire sauce
¼ t	hot sauce
½ t	salt, or to taste
¼ t	dried oregano, crumbled
⅛ t	cayenne
2 T	cold unsalted butter, cold and cut into bits
½ lb	small shrimp
3	scallions, minced
	crusty bread
	lemon wedges

Preheat oven to 450°. Drop garlic into food processor with motor running and mince. Turn motor off. Add lemon juice, black pepper, Worcestershire sauce, hot sauce, salt, oregano, and cayenne and pulse to combine. Add butter and blend until combined well.

Spread shrimp in a shallow baking dish large enough to hold them in one layer and sprinkle with scallions. Drop spoonfuls of butter mixture evenly over top and cover until ready to bake.

MAKE AHEAD: At this point, shrimp can be refrigerated for several hours.

Before baking shrimp prepare the artichokes. In a small sauce pan, add 2 teaspoons oil or butter and briefly sauté the prosciutto. Add artichokes, red bell pepper, and ½ cup chicken broth and heat thoroughly. While heating, begin to bake shrimp. Stir once or twice until shrimp are cooked (don't over cook), about 5 minutes depending on size. Combine shrimp, artichoke mixture and scallions. Serve in soup bowls with crusty bread and lemon wedges.

Seafood

Shrimp and Leek Linguine in White Wine Sauce

SERVES
4

1 lb	small-medium shrimp, peeled and deveined
1¾ C	water
4 T	olive oil
2	large garlic cloves, minced
2-2½ C	leeks (white and pale green parts only from about 2 large leeks), thinly sliced
⅛-¼ C	peperoncini, seeded and thinly sliced
3 T	fresh oregano, minced
3 T	lemon peel, minced
¼ C	dry white wine
½ C	clam juice
¼ C	chicken stock
2 T	fresh lemon juice
12 oz	linguine or angel hair pasta
	fresh parsley, chopped

Heat 2 tablespoons oil in heavy large skillet over medium-high heat. Add garlic and sauté until soft, about 1 minute. Stir in leeks, peperoncini, oregano, and lemon peel. Cover and cook until leeks are soft, about 3 minutes. Uncover, add wine, lemon juice, clam juice, and chicken stock. Increase heat to high for 1 minute. Remove from heat, keep warm. Begin to cook pasta in boiling salted water until al dente.

Meanwhile, heat 2-3 tablespoons of olive oil over medium-high heat in a heavy skillet. Sauté shrimp just until pink. Season with salt and pepper.

Drain pasta reserving about 1 cup liquid. Return pasta to cooking pot, turn heat on, and toss pasta with leek mixture and shrimp. Add reserved liquid if desired. Heat through, season to taste. Serve immediately. Garnish with parsley.

Seafood

Herb Shrimp and Pasta

1 lb	shrimp, peeled and deveined
4 oz	angel hair pasta
1	stick butter
2	cloves garlic, minced
¼ t	salt
¼ C	onion, chopped
1 C	half & half
¼ C	fresh parsley
1 t	fresh dill weed, chopped
⅛ t	pepper

Melt butter; add shrimp, garlic and onions. Cook for 5 minutes or until shrimp are pink. Remove shrimp and set aside. Add half & half, bring to a boil, stirring constantly. Reduce heat to low. Simmer about 15 minutes. Add shrimp, parsley, dill, salt, and pepper. Stir until well blended. Serve over prepared angel hair pasta.

Green Pasta with Shrimp

3 C	water
1 lb	fresh shrimp, unpeeled
2 t	Creole seasoning
1 lb	fresh asparagus

Dressing

1½ C	fresh basil leaves
½ C	olive oil
⅓ C	lemon juice
3	garlic cloves
1 t	salt
¼ t	black pepper
8-12 oz	spaghetti

Make dressing by processing basil, olive oil, lemon juice, garlic, salt, and pepper in a blender or food processor until smooth.

Bring 3 cups of water to a boil: add shrimp and Creole seasoning. Cook for 3 minutes or until shrimp turn pink. Drain and rinse with cold water. Peel shrimp, and devein if desired, set aside. (Or sauté peeled shrimp in Creole seasoning before adding to pasta.)

Snap off tough ends of the asparagus; cut asparagus into 2-inch pieces. Cook spaghetti according to package instructions, adding asparagus the last 3-5 minutes. Drain. Combine shrimp, pasta, and asparagus in a large bowl; drizzle mixture with dressing, tossing gently to coat.

seafood

Shrimp Capellini

1 lb	large shrimp, peeled
½-¾ lb	fresh asparagus, cut on diagonal into 1" pieces
¼ C	sun-dried tomatoes, diced
1 T	garlic, minced
¼ C	olive oil
½ C	white wine
½	stick butter, do not substitute margarine
8-10	leaves fresh basil, thinly sliced
6-8 oz	capellini or angel hair pasta
	Parmesan cheese, grated

Soften sun-dried tomatoes in boiling water (or use oil-packed tomatoes) for 2 minutes. When soft, dice and set aside. Preheat water for pasta. Cook asparagus in salted water until barely tender. Drain and set aside. In oil, sauté shrimp with a little salt, pepper, and garlic until shrimp are pink, 3-4 minutes. Remove shrimp from pan and add to asparagus.

To the oil remaining in the pan, add the diced tomatoes, white wine and butter. Cook until reduced slightly. While capellini is cooking (according to package directions), return shrimp, asparagus, and basil to pan. Heat through. Serve over capellini and divide butter/wine mixture among the serving plates. Sprinkle with grated Parmesan cheese.

Seafood

Tomato, Shrimp, and Fresh Herbs

1 lb	medium shrimp, peeled
1	large garlic clove, finely chopped
¾ lb	ripe tomatoes, coarsely diced, retain juices
¼ C	fruity olive oil
¼ t	crushed red pepper
1 t	dried basil
1 t	dried oregano
	salt and pepper to taste
¼ C	grated Parmesan cheese
8 oz	rigatoni, penne, or linguine
¼ C	fresh flat leaf parsley, chopped coarsely
¼ C	fresh basil leaves, chopped coarsely
1	medium lemon, zest grated

Combine garlic, tomatoes, olive oil, red pepper, dried basil, dried oregano, salt, pepper, and Parmesan cheese in pasta serving bowl. Set aside to warm at room temperature so flavors mingle. Cook pasta as directed.

Cook shrimp separately in a sauté pan. Combine shrimp and drained, cooked pasta in the bowl with the tomato sauce. Sprinkle with parsley, basil, and lemon zest and toss well. Serve at once with extra Parmesan cheese.

Seafood

Creamy Shrimp Creole

1 lb	shrimp, peeled and cleaned
¼ C	flour
⅓ C	oil
1 C	hot water
1	(8 oz) can tomato sauce
½ C	green onions, chopped
½ C	parsley, chopped
¼ C	green pepper, chopped
¼ t	garlic powder
1½ t	salt
½ t	dried thyme, crushed
dash	cayenne pepper
2	bay leaves
1 t	fresh lemon juice
1 t	Creole seasoning
¼ t	black pepper
2 C	cooked rice

Thaw shrimp if frozen (cut large ones in half). Over medium-high heat, blend flour into oil and brown, stirring constantly. Add water gradually and cook until thick and smooth, stirring constantly. Add remaining ingredients except shrimp and rice, cook for 5 minutes. Add shrimp, cover and simmer for 20 minutes. Remove bay leaves. Serve over hot cooked rice.

Seafood

Shrimp and Vegetable Creole

SERVES
8

2 lbs	shrimp, peeled
½ C	butter
1½ C	mushrooms, chopped
1½ C	onions, chopped
1½ C	celery, chopped
1½ C	zucchini, chopped
1½ C	carrots, chopped
1½ t	Creole seasoning
1	(8 oz) can tomato sauce
1	(6 oz) can tomato paste
1	(14 oz) can chicken stock
¼ C	sherry
2 T	flour
2 T	lemon juice
2 C	raw rice

Melt butter in large skillet and sauté vegetables until tender. Add Creole seasoning, tomato sauce, tomato paste, and stock. Cover and simmer 15 minutes.

Cook rice according to the instructions on the package.

Combine sherry and flour; stir into sauce and bring to a simmer. Add lemon juice and shrimp. Cover and simmer 5 more minutes, until shrimp is cooked. Serve over hot rice.

Seafood

Jambalaya: The Big Easy Way

Seasonings

1 t	salt
1 t	black pepper
1 t	cayenne pepper
1 t	white pepper
1 t	gumbo file powder
1 t	dry mustard
½ t	ground cumin
1 t	dried thyme leaves
5-6	bay leaves

Meat and Seafood (a heaping cup of each)

6 oz	smoked ham, diced (or substitute with par-boiled, diced chicken)
6 oz	andouille sausage, diced (or substitute with kielbasa)
6 oz	sweet Italian sausage, crumbled
1 lb	medium shrimp, peeled and butterflied
5 T	butter
2 C	chopped onions
2 C	chopped celery
1½-2 C	chopped bell peppers (using more than one color of pepper adds a nice look)
3-4	garlic cloves, minced
3 C	converted rice
6 C	chicken stock
1	(14 oz) can diced tomatoes, including liquid (seasoned tomatoes are ok)

Seafood

Jambalaya:
The Big Easy Way (Continued)

Mix the seasonings and set aside.

In a very large, heavy skillet or pot, melt butter over high heat. Add the ham and sausages and cook 4-5 minutes, stirring occasionally. Add the onions, celery, peppers, garlic, and the seasoning mix. Stirring frequently, occasionally scraping the bottom of the pot, cook until lightly brown (about 10 minutes).

Stir in the rice (dry) and cook for 5 minutes. Continue to scrape the bottom of the pan periodically. Add chicken stock and diced tomatoes. Stir and bring to a boil. Reduce heat and simmer for 15 minutes.

Add shrimp and stir. Add a splash of white wine if you wish. Continue stirring occasionally, and cook for 5 more minutes. Rice may still be a bit crunchy, but Jambalaya is now ready to be served.

Serve on plates or in bowls, with sliced baguette.

seafood

Crab Cakes

8 oz	lump fin crab meat
6	green onions, diced (use 2" of green stems)
2	egg whites
2 T	capers, drained and rinsed
4 T	flour
⅛ t	cayenne pepper
1 t	lemon juice
1 T	oil
1 T	butter

Gently mix all ingredients above, being careful not to break up the lumps of crab meat. When all ingredients are mixed, form into four patties and sauté in oil and butter until golden brown and firm. Serve with lemon wedges.

Susan's Crab Cakes

1 lb	fresh lump crab meat
4 T	roasted red bell pepper
4 T	green or sweet onion
4 T	cilantro
2 T	light mayonnaise
2 t	Dijon mustard
⅛ t	hot sauce or to taste
⅛ t	Worcestershire sauce
4 T	breadcrumbs
1	egg, beaten

Breading

2 C	fine breadcrumbs
2 T	butter
2 T	oil

Mix crab meat, roasted pepper, onion, cilantro, mayonnaise, Dijon, hot sauce, and Worcestershire sauce, in a large bowl. Mix in ¼ cup breadcrumbs and egg. Shape crab mixture into eight 2½-inch-diameter patties, using scant ½ cup mixture for each. Place 3 cups breadcrumbs in shallow dish. Coat crab cakes in breadcrumbs, pressing to adhere. Melt 1 tablespoon butter with 1 tablespoon oil in heavy large skillet over medium heat. Add 4 crab cakes and cook until golden brown, about 4 minutes per side. Repeat with remaining butter, oil, and crab cakes. Divide among 4 plates. Serve with salsa.

MAKE AHEAD: Can be made up to 6 hours ahead. Cover; chill.

INSIGHT: It is easier to sauté crab cakes if you first place them in the freezer for 10-15 minutes, or chill in refrigerator for an hour. This helps them stay together.

seafood

Roasted Soft-Shell Crabs

Crabs

4	large soft-shell crabs, cleaned
1 T	olive oil
1 T	butter, melted
1	garlic clove, minced

Sauce

2 T	mayonnaise
⅛ t	chipotle chile powder, chipotle sauce, or hot red pepper sauce
1 t	lemon juice

Preheat oven to 500°. Place crabs on foil-lined baking sheet. Combine oil, melted butter, and garlic. Brush over crabs. Roast crabs in oven until crackling and nicely browned, 8-10 minutes.

Meanwhile, prepare sauce by combining mayonnaise, chile powder, and lemon juice; season to taste. To serve, place 2 crabs on each plate. Spoon sauce on side and/or serve lemon wedges.

Seafood

Mary's Deviled Crab

1 lb	fresh crab meat, or pasteurized lump
4	slices bacon
⅓ C	green pepper, chopped
½ C	medium onion, chopped
½ C	butter
1 t	Worcestershire sauce
½ t	hot pepper sauce
3 T	crumbled crackers (like saltines)
	pepper to taste

Pick over crab and set aside. Preheat oven to 350°.

Fry bacon until crisp in large skillet and crumble. Drain fat except for 2 tablespoons. Sauté green pepper and onion in fat until softened. Add butter to pan and stir in Worcestershire and hot sauce. Stir in crackers. Add crab, bacon, and pepper. Mix together gently but well. Put in casserole dish. Bake for 30 minutes.

Seafood

Ginger Scallops with Snow Peas

1½ lb	sea scallops, rinsed and sliced in half horizontally
2 t	sesame oil
3	cloves garlic, minced
1 lb	snow peas, strings removed
1	red bell pepper, cored, seeded and cut into ½" squares
2 T	rice wine or sake
2 t	vegetable oil
2 T	scallion greens, chopped

Marinade

2 T	rice wine or sake
3	slices fresh ginger

Minced Seasonings

2 T	scallions, minced
1½ T	fresh ginger, minced
3	cloves garlic, minced
¼-½ t	red pepper flakes

Sauce

½ C	chicken broth
2½ T	reduced-sodium soy sauce
2 T	rice wine or sake
1 T	Worcestershire sauce
1 T	cornstarch
1 t	sugar

Seafood

Ginger Scallops with
Snow Peas (Continued)

In a medium-sized bowl, combine marinade ingredients, mashing the ginger slices to release their flavor. Add scallops and toss lightly to coat. Cover with plastic wrap and refrigerate for 20 minutes.

Mix minced seasonings in a small bowl and set aside. In another small bowl, combine sauce ingredients and set aside. In a large saucepan, bring 2 quarts water to a boil. Add the scallops and their marinade and cook until opaque, about 30 seconds. Drain, removing ginger, set aside.

Heat wok or a large skillet over high heat; add sesame oil and heat until almost smoking. Add garlic and stir-fry until fragrant, 10-15 seconds. Add snow peas, bell peppers, and rice wine or sake; stir-fry until the vegetables are just tender, 1-2 minutes. Transfer to a dish; set aside.

Return wok or skillet to the heat; add vegetable oil and heat until very hot. Add the reserved minced seasonings and stir-fry until fragrant, 10-15 seconds. Add the reserved sauce mixture and stir until thickened, 1-2 minutes. Add the poached scallops and toss to coat until heated through. Transfer to a platter, sprinkle with scallion greens and serve.

INSPIRATION: This dish is also good served over Chinese noodles or pasta.

Seafood

Sea Scallops Gremolata

Scallops

1 lb	sea scallops
6T	butter
½	lemon, juiced

Gremolata

½	lemon, zest grated
2 T	Italian parsley, chopped
2	small garlic cloves, finely minced

To make the gremolata, combine lemon zest, parsley, and garlic; set aside.

Dry scallops on paper towels and lightly salt each side. Warm a large cast iron skillet over low heat and add 4 tablespoons of butter, increase heat to medium-high. When butter begins to brown, add scallops and sear on both sides, 2-3 minutes per side. Remove the scallops to warm plate, turn heat to medium. Add lemon juice and remaining 2 tablespoons butter, stirring to combine with the browned bits. Spoon over and around scallops and sprinkle gremolata over each.

Seafood

Simple Grilled Lobster Tails

6	lobster tails (fresh or frozen)
	butter, melted

To prepare lobster tails for grilling: Using kitchen shears, cut the top membrane off of the lobster tails and discard. Partially loosen the meat from the shell, leaving the end of the tail attached. Gently lift the loosened tail meat up and rest just on top of the shell. Brush tails with melted butter. When the grill is ready, arrange the tails shell side down 3-4 inches from the heat and cook 8-10 minutes. Brush with butter again, and turn tails over so the meat side is on the grill. Continue to cook 2-4 minutes until the meat is cooked through. Serve with melted butter.

Seafood

MAIN

Mushroom – Stuffed Beef Tenderloin

1	beef tenderloin roast, about 4 lbs, trimmed
6	slices bacon
2 C	mushrooms, chopped
4 T	onion, chopped
2	cloves garlic, crushed
4 T	snipped parsley
2 T	butter, softened
2 t	Dijon mustard
2 T	Parmesan, grated
1½ C	soft breadcrumbs

Make a slit, lengthwise, in the tenderloin from one side to within ½-inch of other side. Set aside. Cook bacon until crisp. Remove bacon and all but 2 tablespoons of drippings. Crumble bacon. Add mushrooms, onion, and garlic to drippings, and cook until onion is tender. Stir in parsley, bacon, and 1 cup of breadcrumbs.

Spoon mushroom mixture down center of the tenderloin. Bring the two sides of the roast up around filling to meet and tie string around roast at 1-inch intervals. Combine butter, cheese, and mustard and spread evenly on roast. Press ½ cup of breadcrumbs into the butter mixture on top and sides of roast. Cover and chill if desired. Preheat oven to 425°.

Bake roast for 35-40 minutes for medium-rare. Remove roast from oven and cover loosely with foil for 10 minutes before serving. Slice into 1-inch thick pieces.

INSPIRATION: This is delicious served with our Horseradish Scalloped Potatoes (see Index).

Beef Tenderloin with Sautéed Mushrooms

1		beef tenderloin, about 3 lbs, trimmed and tied
3		slices bacon, diced
¼ C		butter
2 C		mushrooms, diced
½ C		parsley, minced
¼ C		scallions, minced
2 T		brandy

Preheat oven to 450°. Place tenderloin on a rack in a shallow baking dish. Roast for 30-40 minutes or until desired doneness.

Meanwhile, cook bacon until crisp and reserve. Melt butter and sauté mushrooms, parsley, and scallions until lightly browned. Add brandy and heat through. Stir in bacon.

After tenderloin has rested for 10 minutes, cut on an angle into 1-inch thick slices. Serve, spooning warm mushroom sauce over each slice.

Beef

Beef Wellington

1	beef tenderloin, about 2½ lbs, trimmed
1 T	freshly ground pepper
¼ C	butter, divided
1 C	fresh mushrooms, sliced
1 t	fresh parsley, chopped
½ t	dried basil
½ t	dried tarragon
½ t	dried thyme
½	(17¼ oz) pkg frozen puff pastry sheets, thawed
1	large egg, lightly beaten
	fresh parsley sprigs

Evenly shape tenderloin by tucking small end underneath; tie with string. Sprinkle beef with pepper. Melt 2 tablespoons butter in a large skillet over medium-high heat. Brown beef on all sides. Reduce heat to medium, and cook 30 minutes, turning occasionally or until internal temperature is 125° for rare. Remove from pan; cover and chill.

Melt remaining butter in a clean skillet; add mushrooms, and cook over medium-high heat 2 minutes. Stir in parsley, basil, tarragon, and thyme; cook over medium-high heat until all liquid evaporates. Roll pastry into a 16 x 14-inch rectangle. Spoon mushroom mixture down center. Remove string from beef, and place beef lengthwise in middle of pastry. Bring sides of pastry up, and overlap slightly to form a seam; trim off excess pastry. Reserve all pastry trimmings. Trim ends of pastry and make even; fold over, and seal. Place roast, seam side down, onto a lightly greased baking sheet; brush with beaten egg. Roll out reserved pastry trimmings; cut into decorative shapes, and arrange on top of pastry, as desired. Brush pastry shapes with remaining beaten egg. Cover and refrigerate.

When ready to bake, let stand at room temperature 30 minutes. Preheat oven to 400°. Bake for 20-25 minutes until golden brown. Garnish with parsley.

INSPIRATION: This is an elegant entree which can be prepared in the morning before your dinner party.

Beef

157

Pansy's Style Beef Tenderloin

1	whole beef tenderloin, 3-5 lbs, trimmed and tied salt and freshly ground pepper

Preheat oven to 500°. Rub meat well with salt and pepper. Place meat on foil in roasting pan. Place in oven for 20 minutes. Turn off oven and let sit for 30 minutes. It is very important not to open the oven door to take a peek until the 30 minutes has passed!

Tenderloin prepared this way will be rare in the center and medium-rare toward the ends.

INSIGHT: Roasting times for roasts: Boneless roasts such as a top loin (New York strip) and tenderloin are timed according to their dimensions, not weight. For example, a 2 pound tenderloin will take the same time to roast as a 4 pound.

Beef

Beef Roasted in Salt Crust

1	standing rib roast, 6-8 lbs, trimmed
3 C	kosher salt
¾ C	water

Preheat oven to 325°. In a bowl stir together the salt and ¾ cup water until the mixture forms a slightly stiff paste resembling wet snow. Arrange the rib roast, fat side up, in a roasting pan and coat it completely with the salt mixture, patting the mixture on about ¼-inch thick. Roast the beef in the middle of the oven for 2 hours (about 22 minutes per pound), or until it registers 130° on a meat thermometer for medium-rare meat. Transfer the beef to a cutting board and let it stand for 15 minutes. Remove the crust with a hammer and carve the meat.

Beef

Herb Crusted New York Strip Roast

4-5 lb	New York strip roast, fat trimmed to ¼"
4	garlic cloves
8	fresh sage leaves
4 t	fresh thyme leaves
4 t	olive oil
4 t	sea salt
1½ t	fresh ground black pepper

Drop garlic into running food processor; blend until finely chopped. Add sage, thyme, sea salt, oil, and black pepper; process to a paste. Pat meat dry with paper towels and rub all over with the herb paste. Cover and chill for at least 3 hours.

MAKE AHEAD: At this point, the roast can be refrigerated overnight.

Remove roast from refrigerator 1 hour before roasting. Preheat oven to 450°. Place meat, fat side up, on a rack in a roasting pan. Roast for 15 minutes at 450°. Reduce oven temperature to 350° and roast about 35 minutes until meat thermometer registers 130° in the thickest part for medium-rare, roast about 45-50 minutes for medium, 140°. Remove from oven, cover loosely with foil and let stand for 20 minutes before slicing in ½-inch thick pieces.

INSPIRATION: This is delicious served with our Blue Cheese Vidalia Onions. (see Index)

Beef

Harold's New York Strip

SERVES
1

1	New York strip steak or fillet per person
2	cloves of elephant garlic per person
2	medium yellow onions per person
¼	stick of unsalted butter per person
½ T	green peppercorns in brine per person
	blackening spice

To make compound butter: Place the butter in a bowl and allow to soften at room temperature. Drain peppercorns and add to butter. Mix and place on a sheet of parchment or plastic wrap. Spread butter mixture to a height of roughly 1¼-inches. Roll parchment or plastic wrap around butter and place in refrigerator. This is best done the day before – if making the same day, place the compound butter in the freezer until firm.

Preheat oven to 350°. Toss garlic with olive oil to cover lightly. Wrap loosely in aluminum foil and cook for 30-45 minutes, until garlic is soft. Slice the onions thinly. Heat a skillet to medium and add a teaspoon of butter or oil, sauté onions turning often taking care not to burn. When onions reach a golden brown color, remove and set aside.

Preheat grill. Season steaks lightly with blackening seasoning. When one side is done, reheat garlic and onions. When steaks are finished, place on plate and allow to sit for a few minutes. Squeeze garlic from skin and place cloves on steaks. Top steaks with onions. Slice compound butter and set a disk on each steak. Serve immediately.

Beef

Tenderloin with Dijon Sauce

4	beef tenderloins steaks, approximately 8 ozs each
	salt and pepper to taste
2 T	butter
2 T	shallots, finely chopped
2 T	cognac or brandy
¼ C	chicken stock
3 T	Dijon or coarse mustard
2 T	fresh parsley, chopped

Season beef with salt and pepper. Heat large skillet until very hot. Sear tenderloins for 4 minutes, then turn and cook additional 4-6 minutes or until they reach desired doneness. Remove beef from pan and keep warm.

Melt butter in pan and sauté shallots 2-3 minutes. Add cognac and stock. Bring to a boil and stir in mustard. To serve, pour sauce over beef and garnish with parsley.

INSPIRATION: If you like the charred crust that pan searing provides, but cannot seem to get the inside of your steak done without burning the outside, try this idea: sear your steak in a heavy skillet for 5 minutes per side on medium-high heat. Then remove the steak and wrap in heavy duty aluminum foil, place steak in a preheated 300° oven for 10-15 minutes until steak reaches desired doneness.

Beef

Tenderloin with Charred Tomato Salsa

4	thick tenderloin steaks
2	green peppers
2	red peppers
3	medium tomatoes, cored and seeded
1	large yellow onion
2	large or 3 medium cloves of garlic
1 C	beef stock
⅓ C	red wine
2	ears corn, cooked, or 1 cup frozen corn, thawed
1 C	fresh cilantro or parsley, chopped
	salt
	pepper

Heat a large cast iron skillet to medium. Quarter the peppers, removing the stems, seeds, and the whitish ribs inside the peppers. Peel and quarter the onion. Peel the garlic cloves and trim the ends. Place in heated pan and allow to char on one side. While the vegetables are cooking, core tomatoes and squeeze to remove majority of seeds. Place in pan. Turn vegetables every few minutes to ensure an even char. When vegetables are 50% charred remove from pan. Pour red wine in a pan and reduce by half. Add beef stock and reduce by two thirds. Set aside.

Place vegetables in a food processor. Rough chop the vegetables and add the stock reduction in small amounts until you reach a thin salsa consistency (about that of a hearty soup). Pour into a bowl. Remove kernels from corn and add to salsa mixture, along with the parsley or cilantro.

MAKE AHEAD: The salsa can be prepared early in the day and kept refrigerated. Bring salsa to room temperature before serving.

Season steaks and cook to desired doneness. Allow to sit for several minutes to reabsorb juices. Ladle salsa over steaks.

Beef

Peppercorn Steak

¼ C	cracked pepper
4	rib-eye steaks
1 C	green onions, chopped
1 lb	fresh mushrooms, sliced
¼ C	butter, melted
1 lb	bacon, cooked and crumbled
3 T	Chablis or other dry white wine

Preheat broiler. Pound pepper into both sides of steaks, using a meat mallet.
Set steaks aside. Sauté onions and mushrooms in butter in a skillet until
tender. Add bacon and wine; set aside, and keep warm. Place steaks on a
broiler rack coated with cooking spray; place rack in broiler pan. Broil 4-6
inches from heat 6-8 minutes on each side or to desired degree of doneness.
Remove steaks to a platter, and top with mushroom mixture.

*INSPIRATION: The steaks for this recipe may also be grilled before topping
with sauce.*

Beef

London Broil

1	London broil or top round steak (2½-3 lbs)
⅓ C	soy sauce
⅓ C	red wine vinegar
2 T	honey
2 T	oil
2	cloves garlic, chopped
½ t	dry mustard
½ t	ginger
¼ t	pepper
¼ C	onion, chopped

Cut 3-4 slashes diagonally into London broil across the grain on both sides. Place in a shallow dish or plastic bag. Mix remaining ingredients to make a marinade and pour over meat. Marinate in refrigerator overnight, turning several times. Prepare grill and cook until medium-rare. This cut of meat is most tender if cooked rare to medium-rare. To serve, slice across the grain at an angle in ¼-inch slices.

Beef

Beef Fondue Oriental

1½-2 lb	beef tenderloin
4 C	beef broth
2	cloves garlic, thinly sliced
¼-½ C	dry white wine
1 T	fresh herbs, such as chives

Cut meat into ¼-inch bite-size slices and keep chilled until ready to eat. Prepare your choices of sauces listed on the next page.

Put broth in fondue pot and heat to boiling. Add wine and herbs. Reduce heat to medium to keep broth at an active simmer during cooking.

Spear a piece of meat using a fondue fork and hold in simmering broth until cooked to desired doneness. Transfer meat from fondue fork to dinner plate and dip into your favorite sauce.

INSPIRATIONS: Try cooking pork tenderloin, chicken breast, or shrimp. Use chicken broth in place of the beef broth.

Dipping Sauces

Green Goddess

½ C	sour cream
3 T	mayonnaise
2 T	green onion, chopped

Combine ingredients and chill until ready to serve.

Mustard Sauce

½ C	mayonnaise
1	clove garlic, crushed
1 T	dry mustard
¼ t	hot sauce
dash	Worcestershire sauce

Combine ingredients and chill until ready to serve.

Curry Sauce

½ C	mayonnaise
2 T	milk
1 T	curry powder
¼ t	hot sauce

Combine ingredients and chill until ready to serve.

Horseradish Sauce

3 T	sour cream
3 T	chili sauce
¼ C	onion, minced
1 T	prepared horseradish
1 T	water

Combine ingredients and chill until ready to serve.

Teriyaki Sauce

¼ C	beef consommé
¼ C	dry sherry
¼ C	soy sauce
3 T	lime juice
3 T	brown sugar
1	clove garlic, minced
1 T	fresh ginger

Combine ingredients and heat on low 5 minutes. Serve hot or cold.

Beef

Marinated Flank Steak

1	flank steak, about 1½ lbs
3 T	salad oil
3 T	soy sauce
2 T	ketchup
1 T	vinegar
2	cloves garlic, minced
	ground black pepper

Combine salad oil, soy sauce, ketchup, vinegar, garlic, and pepper. Pour over flank steak. Marinate overnight or all day. Turn steak from time to time. Grill to medium-rare. Slice thinly across the grain.

Beef

Barbequed Beef Brisket

Beef

3-4 lb	beef brisket, trimmed
	onion salt
	garlic salt
	seasoning salt
2 oz	liquid smoke
½ C	lemon juice

Barbeque Sauce

1 C	ketchup
½ C	Worcestershire sauce
	hot sauce to taste
2 T	sugar

Place a beef brisket on large piece of heavy duty aluminum foil in large roasting pan. Sprinkle generously with the three kinds of salt. Pour liquid smoke over meat. Tighten foil over brisket. Be sure no air gets to the meat. Bake at 300° for 1 hour and 15 minutes per pound. Take out of oven and turn sides of foil back, remove all juices except for 1 cup. Pour lemon juice over meat.

Combine ingredients for barbeque sauce and heat in saucepan until pouring consistency. Add barbeque sauce over meat and cook uncovered for an additional 45 minutes. To serve, cut brisket in ¼-½-inch slices against the grain.

Chuck Roast with Peppers and Rice

1	boneless chuck roast, about 3 lbs
1 T	chili powder
1 t	salt
1 t	freshly ground pepper
1 T	oil
2	(14 oz) cans beef broth
2	poblano or green bell peppers, seeded, chopped
1	large red bell pepper, seeded, coarsely chopped
1	yellow onion, chopped
1	(28 oz) can crushed tomatoes
1	chipotle chili in adobo sauce, seeded and finely chopped (optional)
1½ C	long-grain rice, uncooked

Heat oven to 325°. Rub roast on both sides with chili powder, salt, and pepper. Heat oil over medium-high heat in Dutch oven. Add roast; cook until browned on one side, 5 minutes. Turn; cook 5 minutes. Remove to platter.

Add 1 can of the broth to Dutch oven; cook over medium-high heat, scraping bottom of pan to dissolve browned bits. Return roast and any accumulated juices to Dutch oven. Cover; cook in oven 2½ hours.

Remove roast from oven. Stir in peppers, onion, tomatoes, chipotle chili, rice, and remaining can of broth. Return to oven. Cover; cook until meat is tender and rice is cooked, about 30 minutes.

Beef

Beef Burgundy

2 lbs	beef stew meat, cut into ¾" cubes
⅓ C	flour
1 t	salt
¼ t	pepper
3 T	oil
1	medium-large onion, diced
1 C	Burgundy wine
2 t	catsup
2	sprigs parsley
1	small bay leaf
½ t	thyme
⅛ t	garlic powder
1 C	boiling water
2	beef bouillon cubes
½ lb	mushrooms, cut in half or quartered

Combine flour, salt, and pepper. Dredge beef cubes in seasoned flour; brown in oil. Drain oil. Add boiling water to bouillon cubes and stir until dissolved. Add bouillon water, onions, Burgundy wine, catsup, parsley, bay leaf, thyme, and garlic powder to meat. Cover and cook over low heat for 45 minutes. Add mushrooms. Cover and cook 15-30 minutes or until meat is desired tenderness. Remove parsley and bay leaf. Thicken gravy, if desired. Serve over hot rice or noodles. Garnish with chopped parsley.

Beef

Hungarian Goulash

2 lbs	beef stew meat, cut into ¾" pieces
2 T	butter
1 lb	onions, sliced thin
2 t	Hungarian paprika
1	slice lemon
1	clove garlic
1	(14 oz) can stewed tomatoes
1	(14 oz) can beef broth
8 oz	wide egg noodles

Melt butter in heavy pot. Put in meat, paprika and onions; simmer until onions have softened. Chop garlic and add to meat along with the slice of lemon, season to taste. Add tomatoes and beef stock, cover, and simmer until meat is tender, about 1 hour. Thicken gravy with roux of flour and butter. Serve over prepared wide egg noodles.

Stroganoff Ground Beef

½ lb	ground round
¼ C	onion, chopped
1 T	butter
¼ C	fresh mushrooms, sliced
1 T	flour
1	garlic clove, minced
¼ t	salt
⅛ t	pepper
2 T	chili sauce
¼ t	Worcestershire sauce
½ C	beef broth
⅓ C	sour cream
4-6 oz	fine or medium noodles, cooked

In a skillet, melt butter and cook beef and onion together until beef is no longer pink. Stir in flour, garlic, salt, and pepper. Cook and stir over medium heat for 5 minutes. Add mushrooms, chili sauce, and Worcestershire sauce. Reduce heat gently and cook, uncovered, for 10 minutes. Add beef broth. Heat until simmering. Reduce heat. Stir in sour cream just before serving. Heat thoroughly but do not boil. Serve over noodles.

Beef

Lil Cheddar Meatloaves

1	egg
¾ C	milk
1 C	shredded Cheddar cheese
½ C	quick-cooking oats
½ C	chopped onion
1 t	salt
1 lb	lean ground beef
⅔ C	ketchup
½ C	packed brown sugar
1½ t	prepared mustard

Preheat oven to 350°. Beat egg and milk. Stir in cheese, oats, onion, and salt. Add beef and mix well. Shape into 8 loaves. Place in greased 13 x 9 x 2-inch baking dish. Combine ketchup, brown sugar, and mustard; spoon over loaves. Bake uncovered for 45 minutes. If you prefer, omit the ketchup sauce.

Beef

Spaghetti and Meatballs

Meatballs

1½ lb	ground round
2	eggs
¼ C	crushed cornflakes (or finely crumbled breadcrumbs)
½ C	Parmesan, finely grated
2	garlic cloves, minced
2 t	dried oregano
½ t	pepper
1 t	salt

Sauce

3 C	purchased marinara sauce
1½ C	water
1 lb	pasta

In a bowl, crumble ground round. Add remaining meatball ingredients and gently blend. Form 1½-inch meatballs.

Combine marinara sauce and water, bring to a simmer. Add meatballs into simmering sauce. Partially cover and slowly simmer until meatballs are cooked through and tender about 1 hour. Sauce will thicken also. Cook 1 pound of pasta and top with meatballs and sauce.

INSPIRATION: For a meatball sandwich, purchase 6 long French rolls. Split lengthwise and gently press inside of bottom half to compact slightly. Spoon meatballs into depressions. Spoon sauce over meatballs and sprinkle with Parmesan cheese.

Beef

Chili

2 lbs	ground beef
¼ C	cooking oil
2	(16 oz) cans dark red kidney beans, drained
2	large onions, sliced
1	green pepper, chopped
2	garlic cloves, minced
1	(16 oz) canned tomatoes, chopped
1	(8 oz) tomato sauce + a little extra
1½ t	salt
2-4 T	chili powder depending on taste
1	bay leaf
½ t	red pepper
¾ t	oregano
dash	paprika to taste
dash	cayenne to taste

Sauté onions, green bell pepper, and garlic in oil. Add beef and brown. Add everything else. Simmer 1½ hours. Remove bay leaf before serving. For condiments use grated Cheddar cheese, onions, and sour cream. Serve with cornbread.

Beef

MAIN

Southwestern Pork Fajitas with Tomatillo Sauce

2	pork tenderloins, approximately 1 lb each
2 t	ground cumin
2 t	dried oregano
½ t	salt
½ t	pepper
8-12	8" flour tortillas

Sauce

1 lb	tomatillos, husked, rinsed, and quartered
¼ C	chicken stock
2	cloves garlic
½ C	onion
2	serrano or jalapeño peppers, halved and seeded (optional)
½ t	sugar
1 T	lime or lemon juice
	salt and pepper to taste
½ C	cilantro leaves, chopped

Combine cumin, oregano, salt, and peppers. Rub onto all sides of pork. Refrigerate pork 2-6 hours. Meanwhile, or day before, prepare sauce. Begin by simmering tomatillos for 5 minutes in stock. Process garlic, onion, and peppers until chopped. Add cooked tomatillos, sugar, and lime and process until coarsely puréed. Season with salt and pepper. Flavor will be somewhat tart. Reheat before serving, adding cilantro just before serving. Add more stock for thinner sauce.

Grill pork, searing sides. Reduce heat and grill medium-rare to medium. To serve, slice thin. On warm tortillas, place sliced pork and sauce; wrap. Serve with black beans. Tomatillo sauce also goes well with chicken and fish.

INSIGHT: Heat tortillas in a ziploc with all but a small gap zipped. Microwave on high; 4 6-inch corn tortillas take 40 seconds. Leave in ziploc until ready to serve (up to 2 minutes).

Pork, Lamb & Veal

179

Pork Tenderloin Balsamic

2	pork tenderloins, approximately 1 lb each
4	cloves garlic, minced
2 T	fresh rosemary, chopped
1 T	lemon peel
2 t	salt
2 t	pepper
2 T	olive oil
½ C	beef broth
½ C	balsamic vinegar
2 T	butter
2 T	capers (optional)

Preheat oven to 450°. Combine garlic, rosemary, lemon peel, salt, and pepper. Press mix into tenderloin. In large skillet with oven proof handle, heat oil over medium heat. Add tenderloin and cook, turning until browned, 8-10 minutes. Transfer to oven. Roast 10 minutes. Remove pork from pan and keep warm.

Set skillet over high heat and stir in broth and vinegar, scraping up browned meat. Bring to boil and cook until reduced by ½. Whisk in 1 tablespoon of butter at a time. Stir in capers (optional). Cut into thick slices and serve with sauce.

Pork, Lamb & Veal

180

Pork Tenderloin with Herbed Mushrooms

2	pork tenderloins, approximately 1 lb each
	salt and pepper
	flour
4 T	olive oil
¼ C	brandy
10-12 oz	mixed mushrooms, sliced
2 T	butter
2 T	olive oil
2	cloves of garlic, sliced
2 T	fresh chopped parsley
1 T	chopped rosemary
2 T	heavy cream or half & half

Lightly season pork tenderloins with salt and pepper, and then dredge in flour. Heat a 12-inch skillet over high heat. Add 4 tablespoons of olive oil. Sear the pork evenly on all sides. Reduce the heat to med-low. Add brandy, then cover the pan and cook until the internal temperature is 130° or medium-rare. Remove the meat to a platter and cover with foil and a towel. Let rest for about 5-7 minutes.

Using the same skillet, turn heat to med-high and melt the butter and olive oil. Add mushrooms and garlic, sauté for about 4 minutes. Add rosemary, parsley, and cream. Season to taste.

Slice pork into medallions, and pour the herbed mushrooms over the meat.

Pork, Lamb & Veal

Pork Tenderloin in Cream Sauce

2	pork tenderloins, approximately 1 lb each
2 T	butter
1	(15 oz) jar Alfredo sauce
½ lb	button mushrooms, sliced
½ C	dry white wine or vermouth
	salt and pepper

Preheat oven to 325°. Preheat a 12-inch skillet over medium-high heat. Melt 1 tablespoon butter and brown tenderloin. Remove to 9 x 13-inch baking dish and repeat with second tenderloin. Remove to dish. Sauté mushrooms about 3 minutes and divide over tenderloins. Sprinkle with salt and pepper. Deglaze the pan with the wine, add the Alfredo sauce and mix well. Pour over pork. Cover tightly with foil and bake for 1½ hours.

To serve, slice the meat and serve with the sauce.

INSPIRATION: Although this is a long time to cook pork tenderloin, the result produces an extremely tender and moist piece of meat with a delicious sauce.

Pork, Lamb & Veal

Colin's Favorite Sunday Pork Loin

1	pork loin, boneless, 3-4 lbs, leave fat cap on top
2	cloves garlic, minced
½ t	sage
2 t	salt
½ t	nutmeg
2	onions, sliced
2	carrots, sliced
1 C	water
1	jar black currant jelly
1 t	dry mustard

Preheat oven to 325°. Mix garlic, sage, salt, pepper, and nutmeg. Rub all over meat. Place meat in roasting pan with onions, carrots, and water. Bake for 1½ hours, uncovered. Take out and cut fat on top into criss-cross pattern. Spread top of meat with jam mixed with dry mustard. Cook 1 more hour uncovered. Slice and serve with juices and veggies spooned over meat.

Embers One Pound Pork Chop

8	center cut pork chops, about 1 lb each

Marinating Sauce

1¼ C	soy sauce
1¼ C	water
½ C	brown sugar
1 T	dark molasses

Red Sauce

⅓ C	water
14 oz	catsup
12 oz	chili sauce
½ C	brown sugar
1 T	dry mustard

Prepare marinating sauce by mixing soy sauce, water, brown sugar, and molasses. Bring to a boil. Let cool. Put pork chops in a pan with bone-side up. Pour the sauce over the pork chops and let stand overnight in the refrigerator.

The next day, preheat oven to 325°. Take pork chops out of the sauce, place in a baking dish, add ¼ cup of chicken broth and cover tightly with foil. Bake pork chops in oven until tender, about 2 hours.

Combine all red sauce ingredients and bring to a slight boil. After chops are tender, remove from oven and dip in the red sauce. Place chops in a baking pan, cover, and bake for 30 minutes in 350° oven. Finished chops can also be placed on a grill briefly to make the glaze crispy.

Pork, Lamb & Veal

Grilled Pork Chops with Fresh Plum Salsa

2 t	cumin
⅛ t	cayenne pepper
4	center-cut loin pork chops
1 t	salt
½ t	pepper

Mix cumin, cayenne pepper, 1 teaspoon of salt, and ½ teaspoon pepper. Rub on the pork chops. Heat grill or broiler. Cook pork chops, turning once, until browned on both sides, about 10 minutes. Serve immediately with our Fresh Plum Salsa (see index).

Pork, Lamb & Veal

Barbeque Country Style Ribs

5 lbs	country-style pork ribs

Sauce

1 t	salt
½ t	pepper
1 T	paprika
2 t	sugar
1 C	onion, finely chopped
1 T	Worcestershire sauce
1 C	ketchup
¼ C	butter
¾ C	hot water
½ C	lemon juice

Mix all sauce ingredients and boil for 1 minute.

Preheat oven to 350°. Cook the ribs, covered with foil for about 2 hours. Pour the sauce over ribs, cover and cook for another hour.

Pork, Lamb & Veal

Smoked Baby Back Ribs

4 lbs   **baby back pork ribs**
        dry rub (your favorite)

Rub ribs with dry rub and refrigerate several hours. Prepare smoker and when preheated, place ribs bone-side down on rack. Continue to monitor so heat is in the ideal range or about 300°.

If oven-roasting, preheat oven to 300°. Using a broiler pan with rack, put ½-inch water and/or beer in pan; cover with rack and place seasoned ribs bone-side down on rack. Cover tightly with foil and bake for 2 hours. To finish, grill ribs just long enough to brown.

Pork, Lamb & Veal

Kielbasa Marinara

6	links Fresh Market kielbasa or Italian sausage
1	green pepper, sliced
1	red pepper, sliced
½ C	onion, coarsely chopped
1	(16 oz) jar The Fresh Market Marinara Sauce
½ C	water

Preheat oven to 350°. Fry kielbasa in skillet until brown, turning frequently, about 10 minutes. Drain and place links in a 9 x 13-inch baking dish. Arrange red and green pepper and onion around the links. Cover with marinara sauce and water. Bake covered in the oven for 30-40 minutes. Serve with grated fresh Parmesan and your favorite pasta or in a hard roll.

INSIGHT: If you are using the Fresh Market kielbasa, add ½ cup of water or white wine while cooking. Our kielbasa are so lean, this will keep the sausage from sticking to the pan.

Pork, Lamb & Veal

"Hot Brown" Casserole

1 lb	bacon
1½-2 lbs	cooked ham, cubed into ½" pieces
1-1½ lbs	cooked turkey breast, cubed into ½" pieces
9-10	slices firm white bread, cubed
2	sticks butter
1 C	flour
2 qt	milk
1½ t	salt
1 C	Parmesan cheese, grated
1 C	sharp Cheddar, grated
2	medium tomatoes, sliced
	paprika and parsley (garnish)

Preheat oven to 450°. Fry bacon until crisp; drain and crumble, set aside. Cube ham and turkey breast, set aside. Cube bread and place on baking sheet, dot with butter. Toast in oven, turn frequently. Line a 9x13-inch pan with the bread cubes.

Melt butter in a large pan, stir in flour, making "roux"- until golden brown. Scald milk in a large sauce pan. When it comes to a boil, stir it into the flour-butter mixture. Beat with an electric mixer or whisk until smooth and thick. Pour a small amount of the mixture over the bread. Then top with turkey; more sauce; ham; and more sauce until both turkey and ham are used. Then layer the tomatoes. Sprinkle with some of the Cheddar and Parmesan cheese. Cover with foil. Bake in a preheated 300°oven for 1 hour. Remove foil and sprinkle with remaining Cheddar and Parmesan cheese and bacon. Garnish with paprika and parsley.

MAKE AHEAD: This casserole can be made up to one day ahead and kept refrigerated until ready to heat.

Pork, Lamb & Veal

189

"Oven Baked" Rack of Lamb

SERVES
2

1	rack of lamb, trimmed (French cut rib bones 1½" from ends)
1	stick butter, softened
3	large cloves garlic, minced
1 t	coarse ground pepper
	salt

Preheat oven to 400°. Place rack of lamb bone side down. Combine butter and garlic. Coat entire top of lamb with butter and garlic mixture. Sprinkle pepper and salt over lamb. Wrap prepared lamb rack side down with heavy duty aluminum foil. Place lamb in a medium size roasting pan.

Bake for 11 minutes for rare or 12 minutes for medium-rare. Open foil carefully and turn rack so meat side is facing down. Secure foil and bake an additional 11-12 minutes. Remove from oven and heat oven to broil. Let broiler heat for 3 minutes.

Open top of foil carefully so as not to spill any au jus and turn so meat is side up. Cover bones loosely with foil. Broil lamb uncovered approximately 3-4 minutes to brown, watching lamb carefully. Remove lamb from oven and let rest for 5 minutes.

Remove rack of lamb from foil and slice between each rib bone. Arrange rib chops in center plate. Drizzle au jus over chops. Garnish with mint leaves and a dollop of mint jelly.

Roasted Leg of Lamb with Mushroom Sauce

Lamb
1	leg of lamb (6-8 lbs)
2-3	cloves of garlic, cut into slivers
	freshly ground pepper
2-3 T	Worcestershire sauce
2-3 T	fresh rosemary, chopped

Mushroom Sauce
1½ C	beef stock
1 C	chicken stock
½ C	dry red wine
1 T	butter
¼ C	shallots, minced
1 C	mushrooms, chopped

Preheat oven to 325°. Pierce lamb all over and insert slivers of garlic at regular intervals. Rub lamb with black pepper, Worcestershire sauce, and rosemary. Place on a rack in an open roasted pan and roast for 18-20 minutes per pound or until meat thermometer registers 130°F-135°F for medium-rare. Let stand for 20 minutes before slicing.

Prepare sauce while lamb is roasting. Combine beef stock, chicken stock, and dry red wine in a saucepan. Simmer, uncovered, for 15 minutes. Heat a small sauté pan and melt 1 tablespoon butter. Add shallots and mushrooms. Cook until tender. Add mushroom mixture to the stock and simmer gently for 30 minutes, or until flavors are developed. If desired, thicken with 1 tablespoon flour combined with 1 tablespoon butter. Stir in flour mixture gradually to achieve desired consistency. Season to taste with salt and pepper. Keep warm until lamb is ready to slice. Makes 2 cups.

Pork, Lamb & Veal

Butterflied and Marinated Leg of Lamb

Lamb

1   leg of lamb (about 4 lbs), butterflied

Marinade

3 T   olive oil

2 T   soy sauce

2 T   lemon juice

½ t   rosemary, crushed

2 t   Dijon mustard

1-2   cloves garlic, crushed

Mix the marinade ingredients together. Lay the butterflied meat open with boned surface up. For even cooking, slash the lobes in 2 or 3 places by making long cuts about 1½-inches deep. Next, to keep the roast in shape, push a long skewer through the wide top third and another through the bottom third. Rub the smooth underside with olive oil and place on a baking sheet. Rub the marinade into the top (boned side). Cover and marinate for 1-6 hours in refrigerator.

Prepare grill and cook 20 minutes up to 45 minutes depending on heat of grill and desired doneness of lamb. For rosy red, the meat begins to take on resistance to your finger and reads 125° on a meat thermometer. Remove from grill and cover loosely with foil. Let sit for 10 minutes. This will increase the internal temperature about 5°.

To roast in oven, preheat to 375° and roast about 25 minutes for 125° reading.

To carve, start at either end and angle your knife as though slicing a flank steak.

Lamb Shanks

4	lamb shanks, cut in half
	vegetable oil
	salt and pepper
8	cloves garlic, peeled and whole
3 C	liquid, suggest 2 cups dry red wine and
	1 cup of chicken stock

Preheat oven to 325°. In a large oven proof pan with a tight fitting lid, heat oil over medium heat and brown shanks, turning on all sides to brown. Do this in batches so shanks will brown and not steam. Add garlic cloves and liquid stirring up any brown bits. Return shanks to pan along with any juices. Bring to a simmer, cover and put in preheated oven for 2-2½ hours until tender, turning and basting shanks a couple of times during cooking. Serve with rice.

MAKE AHEAD: Shanks may be prepared a day ahead or frozen. Refrigerate to cool and separate fat. Remove fat then freeze or reheat.

Braised Veal Shanks with White Bean Tomato Sauce

5 T	olive oil
2 T	unsalted butter
6	large 2" thick veal shanks (about 4½ lbs), each patted dry and tied securely with kitchen string to keep meat and bone attached
1½ C	onion, chopped
1 C	carrot, chopped
1 C	celery, chopped (optional)
3	garlic cloves, minced
2	fresh thyme sprigs or ¾ tsp crumbled dried thyme
1	(15-19 oz) can white beans, rinsed and drained
1	(28 oz) can plum tomatoes, drained and chopped
1 C	dry white wine
2 C	chicken broth

Gremolata

¼ C	parsley leaves, finely chopped
1 T	freshly grated lemon zest
1½ t	garlic or to taste, minced

Preheat oven to 350°. In a Dutch oven heat 2 tablespoons oil and the butter over medium-high heat until the foam subsides. Brown the veal shanks on all sides for about 8-10 minutes, do this in batches so the meat browns and does not steam, adding more oil as necessary. Transfer to a plate as they are browned. Pour off fat, add the remaining 3 tablespoons oil and cook the onions, carrot, celery, and garlic over medium heat, stirring until the vegetables are softened. Season to taste with salt and pepper.

Return the shanks to the Dutch oven and add the thyme, tomatoes, wine, and broth. Bring the liquid to a boil. Cover and braise in the oven for 3 hours, basting every hour. Transfer the shanks with a slotted spoon to a plate, cover, and keep warm.

Pork, Lamb & Veal

Braised Veal Shanks with White Bean Tomato Sauce
(continued)

Discard the thyme sprigs. Add the beans to the vegetable mixture and heat thoroughly. Adjust seasoning. Return veal shanks and gently reheat.

Make the gremolata by mixing the parsley, zest, and garlic.

To serve, place the veal shanks into individual shallow soup bowls or plates and surround with the bean and vegetable sauce. Sprinkle with the gremolata.

INSPIRATION: If you prefer, omit the beans and serve with mashed potatoes. After the shanks have cooked, purée the vegetable mixture in batches in a food processor. This will make a thick gravy to serve with the veal shanks and potatoes.

Saltimbocca Alla Romano

8	veal cutlets, ⅜" thick slices
	flour
⅔ C	butter, melted
	freshly ground pepper
4	thin slices proscuitto
4	thin slices Fontina cheese
1 t	fresh sage, chopped fine
1	small garlic clove, finely minced
1 C	Frascati, Sauvignon Blanc, or other dry white wine

Garnish
fresh parsley leaves and diced proscuitto

Set eight slices of veal on work board and sprinkle with flour on one side only. Place half of the slices floured side down. Spoon a little of the butter over them and sprinkle lightly with pepper. Place one slice proscuitto and one slice fontina on each of the four slices of veal. Sprinkle with sage, garlic, and parsley, dividing the mixture among the four veal slices. Place remaining four slices on top, floured side up. Press edges together with the tip of a dull knife.

Heat large skillet over medium-high. Add butter. When hot, sauté veal bundles for 5 minutes until browned. Turn and brown 3 minutes. Remove bundles from pan and pour wine into skillet. Stir to loosen any particles.

Return veal to skillet; baste with sauce while simmering for 5 minutes or until done. Season to taste. Garnish with diced prosciutto and parsley.

Sautéed Veal Chops with Mushrooms

4	veal loin chops, 1" thick
2 T	butter
1 T	olive or canola oil
1 lb	fresh mushrooms, sliced
	salt and freshly ground pepper
⅔ C	dry vermouth
½ C	cream
	parsley for garnish

Over medium-high heat, preheat a heavy large skillet that will hold the chops in one layer without crowding, or use 2 smaller skillets. Cover the pan with a thin layer of butter and oil. When hot, add the chops and reduce heat to medium. Brown the chops slowly until lightly browned, about 5 minutes. At this point, in a separate skillet, began to sauté the mushrooms until tender. Turn chops, season with salt and pepper. Increase heat for 2 minutes, and then reduce for last 3 minutes. Turn chops, season lightly. Pour in the vermouth, cover the pan and simmer 1½ minutes more on each side. Veal shops are best cooked so the meat is pink. Remove chops and keep warm.

Rapidly boil sauce for 1 minute, add au jus from sautéed mushrooms and boil 1 minute. Add cream and continue to boil another minute to thicken slightly, then add mushrooms. Add meat drippings from chops, stir and adjust seasoning.

Briefly add veal chops, spooning sauce over each so chops are hot. To serve, place chops on a plate, and cover with mushroom sauce; garnish with chopped parsley.

INSPIRATION: *This recipe also works well using 1" center cut pork chops. Increase cooking time in vermouth to 2 minutes per side.*

Pork, Lamb & Veal

Veal and Mushroom Stew

5-6 T	unsalted butter
2 lbs	veal, cut into 1" cubes
5 T	flour
2 t	Hungarian sweet paprika
1½ t	coriander
	salt and pepper to taste
3 C	canned plum tomatoes, drained, seeded, and chopped
2 C	chicken broth
1½ C	yellow onions, cut in half and then in thin slivered
24	pearl onions (frozen are fine)
2	cloves garlic, minced
¼ C	Italian parsley, chopped plus 1 tbs for garnish
1 T	dried tarragon
	grated zest of 1 orange
¾ lb	small, firm white mushrooms, cut in half
½ C	heavy cream

Preheat oven to 350°. Melt 1-2 tablespoons of butter in a heavy flame proof casserole dish. Over medium heat, add veal and cook turning frequently until sides are no longer pink (do not sear). In a small bowl, combine 2 tablespoons of flour, paprika, coriander, and ½ teaspoon of salt and a ¼ teaspoon of pepper. Sprinkle over veal – cook and stir 5 minutes. Add tomatoes, broth, yellow and pearl onions, shallots, garlic, ¼ cup of parsley, tarragon, and orange zest. Bring to a boil on top of stove. Cover and bake in oven 1½ hours or until veal is tender.

Meanwhile, melt 1 tablespoon of butter in skillet and quickly sauté mushrooms over medium-high heat until golden. Set aside.

Separate stew's liquid by pouring through a strainer placed over a bowl. Save liquid and hold meat in strainer. Return casserole to the stove. Melt 3 tablespoons of butter and sprinkle in 3 tablespoons of flour. Cook for 3 minutes, whisking constantly. Slowly add reserved liquid. Simmer and stir for 5 minutes. Add cream. Adjust seasonings. Return veal to casserole. Add mushrooms and simmer for 5 minutes. Sprinkle with parsley to garnish.

Serve over rice, noodles, or mashed potatoes.

Pork, Lamb & Veal

MAIN

Chicken Mediterranean
a la Riesen

4	chicken breasts, boneless and skinless
1	(14 oz) can chicken broth
4 T	peanut or vegetable oil
1	large sweet onion, sliced
3	large cloves garlic, minced
1 T	dried red pepper flakes
2 T	unsalted butter
16	kalamata olives, pitted and sliced
½ C	dry sherry
2 T	capers, chopped
1¼ t	fresh basil, chopped
3	large, fresh tomatoes, chopped and seeded (or 6 romas)

Preheat oven to 350°. In medium saucepan bring chicken broth to a boil over medium-high heat until reduced to 1 cup. Set aside. Meanwhile, heat 2 tablespoons of oil in a large oven proof skillet over medium heat and add onions, garlic, and red pepper flakes, sautéing until onions are tender. Remove to a bowl and set aside. In a separate bowl, mix together olives, sherry, capers, basil, and tomatoes.

In skillet, over medium-high heat, melt butter and add chicken breasts. Cook 2 minutes on each side to sear meat (do not move during the 2 minutes), then add the chicken broth, and remaining ingredients. Place uncovered in preheated 350° oven and bake for 35 minutes.

INSPIRATION: This recipe is also excellent substituting grouper or red snapper for the chicken. Cooking times and temperatures stay the same.

Poultry

Pecan-Crusted Boneless Chicken Breasts

6	chicken breasts, boneless and skinless
½ C	Dijon mustard
2	eggs
½ C	toasted pecans, finely chopped
1½ C	plain dry breadcrumbs

Wash and thoroughly pat dry chicken breasts. Pound the chicken breasts lightly between 2 sheets of plastic wrap with a flat mallet until they are ½-inch thick. Stir together the mustard and eggs in a flat bowl. Toss together pecans and breadcrumbs in another bowl. Dip chicken in egg mixture and then coat well with pecan and breadcrumb mixture. Bake at 350° for 25 minutes or until lightly browned and cooked through.

Poultry

Chicken with Pear and Mushroom Sauce

1 t	butter
1 t	canola oil
4	chicken breasts, boneless and skinless
	salt and freshly ground black pepper to taste
2 oz	prosciutto, thinly sliced, trimmed of fat, and cut in julienne
2 C	shiitake mushroom caps, thinly sliced (or mix with white mushrooms)
½ C	leeks (white part only), thinly sliced
1	ripe Bosc pear, peeled, cored, and chopped
1½ C	chicken broth
¼ C	dry vermouth
2 T	Madeira
2	scallions, finely chopped
2 T	dried cranberries. chopped
2 T	toasted pecans, chopped

In a large nonstick skillet, heat butter and oil over medium-high heat. Season chicken with salt and pepper and cook until browned and no longer pink inside, 3-4 minutes per side or oven-poach (see Index). Transfer to a plate and keep warm.

Reduce heat to medium; add prosciutto, mushrooms and leeks to skillet and cook, stirring until tender, about 3 minutes. Transfer to a small bowl. Increase heat to high; add pear, chicken broth, vermouth, and Madeira to skillet. Bring to a boil, scraping up any browned bits. Add any juices accumulated on chicken plate. Cook, mashing pears into sauce, until slightly thickened, about 10 minutes. Add prosciutto mixture and cook until heated through.

To serve, thinly slice chicken on the diagonal and fan. Spoon sauce over chicken. Sprinkle scallions, cranberries, and pecans over plate. Serve immediately.

INSPIRATION: This is delicious served around a mound of our Zesty Orange Sweet Potato and Squash (see Index).

Poultry

203

Pat's Mediterranean Style Chicken Breasts

4	chicken breasts, boneless and skinless
½ C	flour
	salt and pepper to taste
1	small red or green bell pepper, cut into narrow strips
2	cloves garlic, minced
1	small onion, chopped
3 T	vegetable oil
3 T	balsamic vinegar
1 t	cornstarch
1 C	chicken broth
½ t	ground black pepper
⅓ C	roma tomatoes, diced (or sun-dried tomatoes packed in oil, drained and diced)
1	small can black or green olive slices, well drained
⅓ C	feta cheese, crumbled

On waxed paper mix flour with salt and pepper. Set aside.

Remove all visible fat from chicken breasts and pound each on both sides to ½-inch thick. Dredge chicken breasts in flour mixture: set aside.

Heat 2 tablespoons oil in 12-inch fry pan over medium-high heat until hot but not smoking. Add chicken breasts in one layer and pan-fry 3 minutes each side. Remove breasts to platter and keep warm. Meanwhile, mix together the balsamic vinegar, cornstarch, chicken broth, and pepper; set aside.

Heat remaining 1 tablespoon oil in fry pan over medium heat, quickly sauté onions, garlic, and green peppers. Carefully add the vinegar mixture and continue stirring and loosening any stuck on particles. Stir mixture until it begins to boil. Add the reserved chicken breasts, tomatoes, and olives. Mix and stir well. Turn chicken pieces over several times in sauce. When mixture comes to boil, reduce heat and cover pan, continue to cook for about 5 minutes or until chicken and vegetables are hot. Check sauce for seasoning.

Serve chicken breasts with vegetable sauce poured over each and topped with crumbled feta cheese.

Parmesan Chicken with Lemon-Caper Sauce

SERVES
6

6	chicken breasts, boneless and skinless
1	stick butter
1 C	breadcrumbs
½-1 C	Parmesan cheese, grated
¼ t	salt
¼ t	pepper
2 T	parsley, chopped

Sauce

6 T	unsalted butter
3 T	capers, drained and rinsed
3 T	lemon juice
2 T	parsley, chopped
	salt and pepper

Preheat oven to 350°. Mix breadcrumbs, Parmesan cheese, salt, pepper, and parsley on a plate. Put melted butter in a bowl. Rinse and dry chicken, then dip in butter and roll in breadcrumbs. Place in a baking dish and bake for about 35-45 minutes, depending on size of chicken breasts; 60 minutes for split-chicken breasts.

Meanwhile, prepare sauce. In a small saucepan, melt butter until slightly brown and nutty. Add capers, cook 3 minutes. Add lemon juice, parsley, salt and pepper to taste. Keep warm and serve over chicken.

Poultry

Oven-Poached Chicken Breasts

4	chicken breasts, boneless and skinless
	salt and freshly ground pepper
	freshly squeezed lemon juice
4 T	butter
	wax paper

Preheat oven to 400°. Lightly season the chicken with salt, pepper, and lemon juice. In an oven proof casserole or shallow pan, heat the butter to bubbling over the stove top. Roll the breasts in the butter and lay flat. Cover with wax paper cut to fit casserole. Place in the middle rack of preheated oven for 6-10 minutes depending on size of breast, or until meat is lightly springy when pressed with your finger.

Remove from pan and serve simply with butter sauce; or substitute poached breast for recipe calling for sautéed chicken breast.

INSPIRATION: An easy method for preparing boneless breasts whether to enjoy as is, create a sauce, or proceed with a recipe calling for sautéed breasts.

INSIGHT: Brining chicken produces a flavorful and moist cooked product. The brining process helps the proteins in the meat absorb water; therefore, the meat is juicier. For boneless chicken breasts, only a 30 minute brining is necessary. Mix together in a nonreactive bowl ¼ cup brown sugar, ¼ cup kosher salt (or 2 T table salt) and 1-quart cold water. Add 4 breasts and refrigerate while preparing the grill.

This process also improves the flavor of pork tenderloins and chops. Because these pieces of meat are larger brine up to 1 hour.

Poultry

Chesapeake Bay Chicken Tenders with Cucumber Sauce

Chicken

1-1½ lbs	chicken tenders
¼ C	cornmeal
2 T	Old Bay seasoning or other seafood seasoning
1½ t	dry mustard
½ t	mace or freshly ground nutmeg
⅛-¼ t	cayenne
2-3 T	corn oil

Cucumber Sauce

1	cucumber, peeled, seeded, and coarsely shredded
½ C	yogurt
¼ C	sour cream
¼ C	fresh chives
¼ t	kosher salt
½ t	freshly ground black pepper
pinch	cayenne (optional)

To make sauce, squeeze shredded cucumber to remove liquid, leaving about ⅔ cup cucumber. Stir cucumber, yogurt, sour cream, chives, salt, pepper, and cayenne together. Taste, adjust seasonings and refrigerate.

Remove tendons from chicken tenders. Mix cornmeal, Old Bay, dry mustard, mace, and cayenne. Coat both sides of chicken with cornmeal mix. In a heavy 10-inch skillet, heat 1½ tablespoons oil on medium-high heat and sauté the chicken for 3 minutes, shaking pan occasionally to keep chicken from sticking. Add ½ tablespoon oil, turn chicken and sauté 2-3 minutes more until cooked. Set chicken on paper towels and keep warm. Sauté remaining chicken, adding 1 tablespoon oil if necessary. Serve with crunchy cucumber sauce or lemon wedges

Poultry

Greek-Style Chicken and Mushrooms

⅛-¼ C	olive oil
4	chicken breasts, boneless and skinless
	flour
1 lb	mushrooms, sliced
4	large garlic cloves, chopped
1 t	dried oregano
1 C	chicken broth
2 T	fresh lemon juice
2 T	dry white wine
	fresh parsley, chopped

Heat olive oil in heavy large skillet over medium-high heat. Sprinkle chicken with salt and pepper; dust with flour. Add chicken to skillet; sauté until brown, about 2 minutes per side. Using tongs, transfer chicken to plate, add chicken stock if necessary to deglaze the pan. Add mushrooms, garlic, and oregano to same skillet. Sauté until mushrooms brown, about 5 minutes. Add broth, lemon juice, and wine and boil until sauce is slightly reduced, about 5 minutes.

Add chicken to sauce. Reduce heat and simmer uncovered until chicken is cooked through, about 2-4 minutes per side. Season with salt and pepper. Transfer chicken and mushroom sauce to platter. Sprinkle with parsley.

INSPIRATION: This is delicious served with our Spinach and Feta Rice (see Index).

Chicken Pizzaiola

4	chicken breasts, boneless and skinless
1	(7 oz) can plum tomatoes
¼ t	salt
dash	pepper
1 T	oil
1 T	capers, rinsed and drained, then smashed
¼ t	chopped oregano
4	slices fontina cheese
3 oz	bacon

Preheat oven to 375°. Put tomatoes in a bowl along with the liquid. Mash with a fork, season with salt and pepper. Add the oil, capers, and oregano. Lay in an oiled ovenproof dish (or line with foil). Season with salt and pepper. Cover with the slices of cheese. Lay the bacon slices on top of the cheese. Top with the tomato mixture. Bake for 30 minutes.

Poultry

Marinated Raspberry Chicken

4	chicken breasts, skinless and boneless
¼ C	stone-ground Dijon-style mustard
2 T	brown sugar
3 T	water
1 T	raspberry wine vinegar
1 t	olive oil
2	cloves garlic, minced
¼ t	pepper

Combine mustard, brown sugar, water, raspberry wine vinegar, olive oil, garlic, and pepper. Pour marinade over chicken, coating well. Cover and refrigerate for 2 hours or overnight.

Remove chicken from marinade. Heat marinade to boil and remove from heat to cool. When marinade has cooled, grill chicken over medium hot coals, basting occasionally with marinade.

INSPIRATION: This chicken makes an excellent chicken salad. Cut chicken into pieces and add mayonnaise, chopped celery and toasted slivered almonds.

Grilled Lime Chicken with Black Bean Sauce

4	chicken breasts, skinless and boneless
3 T	fresh lime juice
1 T	vegetable oil
¼ t	ground red pepper
3	cloves garlic, crushed
1 C	water
½ C	red bell pepper, diced
1 T	red onion, chopped
1 C	black beans, drained
½ C	unsweetened orange juice
2 T	balsamic vinegar
¼ t	salt
⅛ t	freshly ground black pepper
1	clove garlic, crushed
	fresh cilantro sprigs (optional)

Combine lime juice, vegetable oil, red pepper, and garlic in a large zip-top heavy-duty plastic bag. Add chicken; seal bag, and marinate in refrigerator 8 hours, turning bag occasionally.

Bring water to a boil in a small saucepan; add bell pepper and onion. Cook 30 seconds; drain. Plunge into ice water; drain well. Set aside.

In a food processor add beans, orange juice, balsamic vinegar, salt, pepper, and garlic. Process until smooth. Pour into a saucepan; cook over medium-low heat until heated.

Remove chicken from bag and grill over medium-hot coals. Cook 8-10 minutes on each side or until chicken is done. To serve, divide bean mixture onto each of 4 plates. Place chicken breast on top of sauce; top each with 2 tablespoons bell pepper mixture or a fresh tomato salsa. Garnish with fresh cilantro.

Poultry

Easy Chicken Cordon Blue

4	chicken breasts, boneless and skinless, seasoned lightly with salt
4	slices good quality ham
4	slices Swiss cheese
1	beaten egg
½ C	breadcrumbs
1 C	white wine – good quality
1	(10 oz) can cream of mushroom soup

Preheat oven to 350°. Flatten chicken breasts. Place ham and cheese on top of chicken and roll up. Secure with toothpicks. Dip into beaten egg and roll in breadcrumbs. Lay in baking dish. Mix in separate bowl mushroom soup and wine. Spoon mix around the chicken and bake covered for 30 minutes. Take cover off and bake an extra 15 minutes. When serving the chicken remove toothpicks and add sauce to the top.

MAKE AHEAD: Can be assembled earlier in the day and refrigerated until ready to bake.

Poultry

Chicken for a Winter Night

5	slices of bacon
	butter if needed
3	whole boned chicken breasts, cut in 2" chunks
½ C	flour mixed with ½ tsp salt and pepper
4	medium red potatoes, cut into chunks
2	cloves garlic, minced
1	large onion, chopped
½ t	thyme
⅔ C	chicken broth
½ C	fresh parsley, chopped (optional)
½ C	dry white wine

Preheat oven to 350°. Cut bacon in ½-inch pieces and cook until crisp. Remove from skillet. Coat chicken in flour mixture. Brown chicken in bacon fat. Do not crowd chicken in the pan. Add butter if you need more fat. As chicken browns, put in 3-quart casserole dish. Add potatoes, onions, and garlic to skillet and brown lightly. Add to chicken. Put thyme and broth in skillet. Heat and scrape crust from skillet. Pour evenly over chicken and scatter bacon pieces on top.

Cover and bake for 40 minutes. Add parsley and wine. Uncover chicken and increase heat to 425°. Bake 15 minutes longer or until potatoes are tender.

Poultry

Balsamic BBQ Chicken

2	chicken breasts with the bone
½	stick butter
1 C	sugar
1-2 T	red pepper, crushed
1-2 C	balsamic vinegar or enough to cover the chicken (inexpensive variety is fine)

Melt butter, add the vinegar, red pepper, sugar and bring to a boil. Wash off chicken and add it to the sauce. Reduce heat to low; cover and slowly simmer for about 45 minutes. Allow the vinegar, sugar, and butter to absorb into the chicken. The chicken will fall off the bone.

Barbecued Chicken Thighs

8	boneless chicken thighs
	onion slices
	smoked seasoned salt
	pepper

Sauce

½ C	ketchup
¼ C	canola oil
½ C	maple syrup
¼ C	vinegar
2 T	yellow mustard

Preheat oven to 375°. Place chicken in baking pan. Tuck thick onion slices around the chicken. Sprinkle with smoked seasoned salt and pepper. Bake chicken, uncovered for 25 minutes. Pour sauce over chicken and bake for 25 minutes longer.

Poultry

Greek-Style Chicken

4	chicken leg quarters with skin
¼ C	olive or salad oil
2 t	garlic, minced
	juice of 2 lemons
1 T	oregano
½ t	salt
⅛ t	fresh pepper

Wash and trim chicken of excess fat. Combine remaining ingredients and marinate chicken overnight.

Preheat oven to 350°. Place chicken, skin side down, on broiler rack over broiler pan. Bake 1¼ hours, turning skin side up after 45 minutes. Chicken may be grilled.

Poultry

Dorothy's Roasted Chicken

3½ lb	roasting chicken (a larger chicken may be used)
2	lemons, cut up
3	bay leaves
¼ C	olive tapenade
1 T	oregano
1 T	paprika
1 t	kosher salt
1 T	black pepper
1 T	garlic powder

Preheat the oven at 450°. Stuff chicken with the lemons and bay leaves. Rub chicken with olive tapenade, rubbing as much as possible under the skin, and sprinkle the remaining ingredients onto the chicken. Place the chicken on a roasting rack. Once in the oven, reduce the oven to 350° and cook for 20 minutes per pound or until internal temperature is 180°.

Poultry

Cheesy Chicken and Artichoke Bake

1	(14 oz) can chicken broth, defatted
1-1½ lbs	chicken breast, boneless and skinless
½ C	onions, chopped
1	clove garlic, minced
¾ C	evaporated skim milk
2 T	dry white wine
2 T	cornstarch
⅓ C	Parmesan cheese, grated
¼ t	thyme
¼ t	salt
⅛ t	ground white pepper
1	(14 oz) can artichoke hearts (with juices)
2 C	fresh mushrooms, sliced

Bring the broth to a simmer in a large skillet. Carefully add the chicken. Cover and simmer for 10-15 minutes or until the chicken is no longer pink. Reserve ¾ cup broth. Cut the chicken into bite-size pieces and set aside.

Preheat oven to 350°. In a medium saucepan heat 1 teaspoon oil. Add the onions and garlic. Cook and stir over medium heat until the onions are tender and translucent. Stir in the reserved broth and milk. Stir together the cornstarch and wine until smooth. Using a wire whisk, slowly stir the cornstarch mixture into the broth mixture. Cook and stir over medium heat until the mixture comes to a boil. Reduce the heat. Cook and stir for 1 minute more. Stir in the thyme, salt, and pepper. Adjust seasoning.

Lightly spray a 2-quart casserole with no-stick spray. Place the chicken in the dish and sprinkle with parmesan cheese. Drain the artichokes and reserve the juices. Cut the artichokes in half and arrange them around the chicken. Pour the sauce over the chicken and artichokes. Bake for 25-30 minutes or until heated through. Meanwhile, add 2 tablespoons of reserved artichoke liquid to a medium skillet. Add the mushrooms. Cook and stir until tender. Before serving the casserole, top with the mushrooms.

Moroccan Chicken with Golden Rice

1	(7 oz) pkg yellow rice
1 C	seasoned flour
3 T	olive oil, divided
3 T	butter, divided
4	chicken breasts, boneless and skinless
1 T	shallots, chopped
4 T	capers
1	lemon, sliced into circles
¾ C	coconut milk
½ t	sugar

Prepare rice according to directions on package. When cooked, set aside and keep warm.

Preheat oven to 375°. Dredge chicken in flour. In large skillet, heat 2 tablespoons olive oil and 2 tablespoons butter over medium-high heat. Add chicken breast. Brown well on both sides. Remove from pan. Set aside. Pour excess grease from skillet. Wipe clean with paper towel. Add remaining olive oil and butter to skillet. Heat over medium-high heat. Add shallots and capers. Sauté for 30 seconds. Add lemons, coconut milk and sugar. Bring to a boil for about 1 minute.

In an oven proof casserole dish, place yellow rice. Place chicken on top of rice. Pour coconut milk mixture over top. Bake for about 15 minutes or until chicken is cooked through. Serve hot.

Poultry

Chandler's Chicken and Rice

5	boneless chicken breasts, cooked and shredded
1	(6 oz) box wild rice mix, cooked according to instructions
1 C	cheddar cheese, grated
1 C	Swiss cheese, grated
1	(10 oz) can cream of mushroom soup
1 C	onion, chopped
½ C	green pepper, chopped
½ C	red pepper, chopped
½ C	celery, chopped
6 T	butter
4	lemons, thinly sliced
	salt and fresh ground pepper to taste

Preheat oven to 375°. Mix chicken, rice, cheddar cheese, Swiss cheese, and mushroom soup; set aside. Sauté onions, peppers, and celery in butter till soft. Add to chicken mixture and season to taste. Put in a 9 x 13-inch casserole dish. Place lemon slices on top. Sprinkle with more fresh ground pepper. Cover with foil and bake 375° for 20 minutes or until heated all the way through.

INSPIRATION: You could substitute 2-3 pounds of shrimp for the chicken in this dish.

Poultry

220

Chicken and Wild Rice Casserole with Dried Cranberries

1⅓ C	(8 oz) wild rice, cooked
4½ T	butter
5 T	flour
3½ C	chicken broth
3-4 T	shallots, minced
1 lb	mushrooms, sliced thin
1 C	heavy cream
⅛ t	freshly grated nutmeg
1½ T	lemon juice
3 C	cooked chicken, cubed
1 C	dried cranberries or cherries

Preheat oven to 400°. In a heavy saucepan melt 3½ tablespoons of butter over moderately low heat. Add flour, and cook, whisking for 3 minutes. Add the broth, bring the mixture to a boil, then simmer, whisking occasionally, for 15 minutes. While the sauce is simmering, in a skillet cook the shallots and the mushrooms in the remaining 1 tablespoon of butter over moderate heat, stirring occasionally, until most of the liquid is evaporated. Add the mushroom mixture to the sauce and stir in the cream, nutmeg, the lemon juice, the chicken, the cranberries or cherries, rice, salt and pepper to taste.

Transfer mixture to a 13 x 9-inch baking dish and bake the casserole, covered, in the middle of preheated oven for 20 minutes. Uncover, bake an additional 15-25 minutes, or until most of the liquid has been absorbed. Garnish casserole with the additional cherries or cranberries.

MAKE AHEAD: This casserole can be made up to one day in advance and kept refrigerated. Bring casserole to room temperature before re-heating. Cover and bake in a preheated 350° oven for 15-20 minutes, or until casserole is heated through.

INSPIRATION: For added flavor, you can marinate the chicken breasts in lemon juice, garlic and Dijon mustard and grill the chicken the day before using in the casserole or prepare our Marinated Raspberry Chicken (see Index).

Poultry

221

Chicken Sausage with Fennel

4	chicken breasts, boneless and skinless
1	small sweet onion, minced
3 T	fine, dry breadcrumbs
2 t	fennel seeds
1 t	salt
1	medium clove garlic, minced
1	small onion, chopped
½ t	dried crushed red pepper
¼ t	ground nutmeg
4	hoagie rolls, split
¼ C	Dijon mustard
	purple onion slices
	plum tomato slices
	leaf lettuce

Pulse chicken in a food processor 6 times or until ground. Add onion and next 7 ingredients; process 2 minutes. Shape into 8 patties. Cook patties in a lightly greased nonstick skillet for 5 minutes on each side or until done. Spread cut sides of rolls evenly with mustard. Place onion and tomato on bottom halves; top each with 2 sausage patties and lettuce. Cover with top halves.

Poultry

Black and White Bean Chili

2 T	oil
1 C	onions, chopped
1	garlic clove, minced
¼ C	flour
1-2 t	chili powder
½ t	cumin
2 C	milk
2	(9 oz) pkg frozen white corn
1	(15.5 oz) can northern beans, drained and rinsed
1	(15 oz) can black beans, drained and rinsed
1	(14.5 oz) can chicken broth
2 C	cooked chicken, cubed
1	(4 oz) can green chiles, undrained and diced
¼ C	fresh cilantro, chopped
6	cilantro sprigs for garnish

Heat oil in Dutch oven or large saucepan over medium-high heat until hot. Add onions and garlic; cook until onions are tender. Stir in flour, chili powder, and cumin. Gradually stir in milk. Add remaining ingredients except cilantro; stir to combine. Bring to a boil. Reduce heat; simmer 15 minutes. Stir in chopped cilantro.

Poultry

MAIN

Herbed Fusilli with Roasted Vegetables

1	red bell pepper, cut into 1" squares
¼ lb	green beans, cut into 1" pieces
2	carrots, cut into ¼" diagonal slices
10	Brussels sprouts, quartered
1	onion, cut into ¼" slices
½ C	olive oil
¾ t	salt
¼ t	fresh ground pepper
1	clove garlic, minced
3 T	red wine vinegar
¾ lb	fusilli pasta
¼ C	mixed herbs – basil, tarragon, parsley, and chives, chopped
½ C	Parmesan cheese, grated

Heat the oven to 450°. In a large bowl, toss the red pepper, green beans, carrots, Brussels sprouts, and onion with 2 tablespoons of the oil, the salt, and the pepper. Spread the vegetables in one layer on a baking sheet and roast until browned and tender, 15-20 minutes. Stir the vegetables 2 or 3 times during cooking. Return the vegetables to the bowl and toss them with the garlic and vinegar.

Meanwhile, in a large pot of boiling, salted water, cook the fusilli until just done, according to the package. Drain. Toss with the remaining 6 tablespoons oil, the herbs and cheese. Top with the roasted vegetables and toss before serving.

INSPIRATION: *Eliminate the pasta, roast the vegetables and toss with the herbs, serve as an accompaniment to a meat entrée.*

Pasta

Tomato-Butter Pasta with Toasted Walnuts

1 lb	linguine
1 C	walnuts, chopped and toasted
⅓ C	extra-virgin olive oil
2	carrots, sliced
½	small red onion, chopped
3	green onions, chopped
1	(28 oz) can whole tomatoes, chopped
2-3 t	minced garlic (fresh or from a jar)
¾ C	chicken broth
½ C	white wine
½ t	crushed red pepper
1	bay leaf
1½	sticks unsalted butter
1 C	fresh minced parsley
	salt and pepper to taste

Toast chopped walnuts in a dry saucepan over medium heat until they just begin to color. Remove and set aside.

In a medium size stock pot, heat the olive oil and add the carrots, red onion, green onions, and cook for about 5 minutes. Add tomatoes, with their juice, to vegetable mixture. Then add the chicken broth, white wine, red pepper, and bay leaf. Cover, bring to a simmer and cook for about 20 minutes. Add butter to tomato mixture and allow to melt, add parsley. Remove bay leaf. In a food processor or a blender, puree the sauce until almost smooth. Return sauce to pan and keep warm.

Meanwhile, boil water for the pasta and add 2 tablespoons salt before adding the pasta. Cook according to package instructions.

Spoon sauce over pasta and garnish with toasted walnuts. Add parsley if desired.

INSPIRATION: Sauce can be made ahead of time and reheated. This sauce also freezes well.

Pasta

Roasted Sausages with Pasta, Peppers, and Pesto Sauce

1½ lb	Italian sausages
2 T	olive oil
1	large red bell pepper, slivered
1	(12 oz) jar button mushrooms, sliced or 8 oz fresh mushrooms
1	medium sweet onion, cut into strips
¾ C	prepared pesto sauce
	salt and pepper to taste
1 lb	linguine, cooked and drained
⅓ C	Parmesan cheese, grated

Cook sausages about 20 minutes or until cooked through. Cut into ½-inch thick slices. Heat olive oil in a large skillet; sauté peppers, mushrooms, and onions until tender. Add pesto sauce and sausage. Toss about 3 minutes to warm through. Season to taste with salt and pepper. Toss with linguine and serve with a sprinkling of Parmesan cheese.

Pasta

Sausage and Spinach Penne Pasta

1 lb	sweet or hot Italian sausage
1	(16 oz) bag fresh spinach
4 T	olive oil
3-4	cloves garlic, sliced very thinly
	salt
	red pepper flakes to taste
¼ C	Romano cheese
1 lb	penne pasta

Take sausage meat out of casings. Sauté until cooked and then place on paper towel lined plate to absorb fat. Keep warm.

Heat olive oil in pan; add sliced garlic and sauté for 1 minute. Add washed spinach leaves and sprinkle with salt and crushed red pepper. Simmer 4 minutes until cooked and stems are soft. Add sausage, toss to mix. Remove from heat.

Meanwhile cook penne according to package directions, drain. Toss spinach mixture, cheese, and pasta together. Top with additional cheese before serving.

Pasta

Cajun Pasta

½ C	butter
¾ C	onions, chopped
½	medium green bell pepper, chopped
½	medium red bell pepper, chopped
½	stalk celery, chopped
½ C	flour
1	(14 oz) can tomato purée
1	(14 oz) can tomatoes, chopped
2 C	half & half
3 oz	andouille sausage
2 oz	Tasso or Westphalian ham
2 t	Creole seasoning
	salt and pepper
¾ C	green onions, tops included
¼ C	parsley
1½ oz	Parmesan cheese
½ lb	small shrimp
1 lb	angel hair pasta

Prep all vegetables – finely chopping green onions and parsley; set aside. Prep meats – coarsely chop all. Shrimp should be shelled and kept refrigerated.

Melt butter over medium heat and sauté onion, bell peppers, celery until limp (about 5 minutes). Add flour, and stir for a few minutes, do not over brown. Add tomato purée, chopped tomatoes, half & half, and meats (DO NOT add shrimp yet) stirring constantly, bring to a simmer. Add Creole seasoning, salt and pepper to taste. Add green onions, parsley, and cheese. Add shrimp and stir for a minute. Turn heat off.

Cook angel hair pasta al dente. Drain the pasta well. Place pasta on plate; top with sauce and garnish with extra green onions and parsley.

INSPIRATION: *Instead of shrimp, chopped chicken or ham may be used. Instead of andouille sausage, smoked sausage may be substituted. Fresh chopped garlic can be added with onion to sauté.*

Pasta

Lemon Garlic Chicken Over Angel Hair

SERVES
4

½	stick butter
4	chicken breasts, skinless and boneless
4	cloves garlic, crushed
½ C	chicken broth
½ C	white wine
3 T	lemon juice
	basil or oregano to taste

Melt butter in a large skillet or 2 smaller ones over medium-high heat. Season rinsed and dried chicken breasts with salt and pepper. Sauté 3-4 minutes on each side to brown, adding garlic during last 2 minutes. Add broth, wine, and lemon juice; bring to a boil. Reduce heat, cover, and simmer 15-20 minutes until chicken is barely pink in the center. Remove from pan and keep warm. Turn up heat (combine liquids from 2 skillets) and bring to a boil, add herbs and simmer for 2 minutes. Season to taste.

Meanwhile, cook angel hair pasta until al dente, about 3 minutes. Drain and toss into liquid-herb sauce. To serve, divide pasta among plates. Top with your choice of prepared vegetables. Add chicken breasts either whole or sliced and fanned along edge of pasta.

INSPIRATION: Top the pasta with 2 cups of peas or fresh asparagus or 2 cups diced tomatoes tossed with 3 tablespoons fresh basil, 2 tablespoons olive oil, salt and pepper. You may also garnish with feta cheese before serving.

Pasta

232

Manicotti

8	eggs, well beaten
1 C	water, cold
1 C	flour
1 t	salt
	tomato sauce (see Cannelloni in Index)

Filling

2 lbs	ricotta cheese
2	large eggs, beaten
8 oz	mozzarella cheese, grated
1 T	parsley
	salt and pepper to taste

To beaten eggs, add water, salt, and flour. Mix well. Let stand 30 minutes. Mix all filling ingredients together, cover and refrigerate.

To prepare manicotti, which resemble a crêpe, melt just enough butter to cover small skillet or crepe pan very lightly. Pour batter as for pancakes but very, very thin. Allow to set. Turn and heat for ½ minute more. Lay prepared crêpes on wax paper or kitchen towel until ready to fill.

Preheat oven to 325°. Add tomato sauce to a 9x13-inch baking pan, just covering the bottom of the pan with the sauce. Using about a tablespoon of the filling mixture, fill each manicotti. Place manicotti seam side down in the pan, forming a single layer. Cover with more tomato sauce. Bake for 45 minutes until bubbly.

INSPIRATION: *Purchased tomato sauce can be used instead of homemade if you are in a hurry. Choose a mild smooth sauce to compliment the delicate flavors of the manicotti and cheese.*

Pasta

Cannelloni

Tomato Sauce

4 T	olive oil
1 C	onion, finely chopped
4 C	canned tomatoes, coarsely chopped (reserve liquid)
6 T	tomato paste
2 t	dried basil
2 t	sugar
1 t	salt
	black pepper

Meat Filling

2 T	olive oil
¼ C	onion, finely chopped
1 t	garlic, minced
1	(10 oz) pkg frozen chopped spinach, thawed, squeezed dry
1 t	butter
1 lb	ground round beef
8 T	Parmesan cheese, grated
2 T	whipping cream
2	eggs, lightly beaten
1½ t	oregano
	salt and pepper

Bechámel Sauce

4 T	butter
4 T	flour
1 C	milk
1 C	whipping cream
1 t	salt
⅛ t	white pepper

Pasta

Cannelloni (Continued)

1 lb	box lasagna noodles
4 T	Parmesan cheese, grated
2 T	butter, cut in pieces

Tomato Sauce: Heat oil in a 2 or 3-quart saucepan until a light haze forms over it. Add onions and cook until soft. Add tomatoes with liquid and other remaining ingredients. Reduce heat to very low and simmer for 40 minutes with pan partially covered. Stir occasionally. Blend tomato mixture in blender and taste for seasoning. Correct if necessary. Makes 3 cups.

MAKE AHEAD: This sauce can be made up to 3 days ahead of time.

Make Filling: Heat oil in a skillet. Add onion and garlic. Cook over moderate heat, stirring frequently, for 7-8 minutes until soft. Stir in spinach and cook 3-4 minutes, stirring constantly. When all the moisture has cooked away, transfer to a large mixing bowl. Melt butter in same skillet and lightly brown meat, stirring. Add meat to spinach mixture. Add cheese, cream, eggs, and oregano. Mix and season with salt and pepper.

Bechámel Sauce: In a heavy 2 or 3-quart saucepan melt butter over moderate heat. Remove from heat and stir in flour. Add milk and cream all at once, stirring constantly with whisk. When the sauce comes to a boil and is smooth, reduce heat. Simmer, still stirring, for 2-3 minutes or until sauce is thick enough to coat the whisk wires heavily. Remove from heat and season with salt and pepper.

To assemble cannelloni, cook lasagna according to package instructions. Cut each whole lasagna noodle into 3 equal sections. Pour a light film of the tomato sauce into 2 (10 x14-inch) shallow baking dishes. Place a tablespoon of the meat filling on the bottom third of each of the pasta rectangles and roll them up. Lay the cannelloni side by side, seam-side-down, in 1 layer on the tomato sauce. Pour bechámel sauce over cannelloni and spoon rest of the tomato sauce on top. Sprinkle the Parmesan cheese over the assembled cannelloni and dot with butter.
Preheat oven to 375°. Bake cannelloni uncovered for 20 minutes or until cheese is melted and sauce is bubbling.

INSPIRATION: The finished cannelloni can be refrigerated up to 24 hours before baking, or it can be frozen up to 3 months.

Pasta

235

Chicken Lasagna

10-11	lasagna noodles
1	(10 oz) can cream of chicken soup
1 C	chicken broth
6 oz	cream cheese, softened
1 C	sour cream
½ t	salt
½ C	Swiss cheese, shredded
1 C	Cheddar cheese, shredded
¼ C	parsley
2 C	mozzarella cheese, shredded
3 C	cooked chicken, chopped

Cook lasagna noodles according to package directions. Drain. In a bowl combine soup and broth. Stir until smooth; set aside. In a separate bowl, combine cream cheese, sour cream, salt, Swiss cheese, and parsley. Set aside.

In a greased 13 x 9 x 2-inch dish, first layer noodles, then half of the cream cheese mixture, half of the cooked chicken, and then half of the soup mixture. Sprinkle on half of the Cheddar cheese and mozzarella. Repeat those steps again (reserving the shredded cheeses) and finish with a layer of noodles. Cover with remaining mozzarella and Cheddar cheese. Bake at 375° for 25 minutes or until bubbly. Let stand 10 minutes before serving.

INSPIRATION: You could add chopped onion and/or chopped green pepper to the cream cheese mixture.

Pasta

Vegetable Lasagna

1	(16 oz) box no boil lasagna noodles
4 C	homemade tomato sauce or The Fresh Market marinara sauce
1 C	onion, coarsely chopped
5 oz	fresh baby spinach
1	large eggplant, peeled, sliced and cut into ½" chunks
2	cloves garlic, finely chopped
4 T	olive oil
4 T	pesto (2 tbsp if using a full-flavored sauce), divided
	salt and pepper to taste
1	slice lemon
12 oz	ricotta cheese

Preheat oven to 375°. After slicing eggplant, sprinkle with salt and arrange on paper towel to drain for about 20 minutes. Take ¼ of chopped garlic and sauté with one tablespoon of olive oil in a 12-inch saucepan that conducts heat well. When cloves turn light yellow, about one minute, add spinach and sauté quickly 2-3 minutes. Lightly salt when finished, remove from pan and set aside. Sauté onions and remaining garlic in 3 tablespoons of oil for 2 minutes over medium-high heat, then add eggplant. As you sauté, keep folding onions and eggplant together, so that eggplant cooks evenly and doesn't brown. Cook until eggplant is well-done and some seeds become apparent. Squirt small lemon slice over mixture (and a little lemon rind if you wish).

Mix together ricotta cheese and 2 tablespoons pesto sauce and set aside.

Spoon enough tomato sauce in 9-inch baking pan or dish to cover the bottom. Then put in your first lasagna layer, followed by one layer of eggplant/onion mixture. Mix pesto to taste with remaining tomato sauce and spoon about 1 cup sauce over mixture. Put second layer of lasagna on and repeat process with eggplant/onions and sauce. Put third layer of lasagna on, add spinach, then add ricotta cheese mix, and top with remaining tomato sauce. Cover with foil and bake for 55 minutes. Remove foil, check if noodles are done, and bake an extra 10 minutes, if needed. Let stand for 5 minutes before serving.

Pasta

237

Spinach Lasagna

1 lb	ricotta or small cured cottage cheese
2 C	mozzarella cheese, shredded
1	egg
1	(10 oz) pkg frozen, chopped spinach, thawed and well drained
1 t	salt
¾ t	oregano
⅛ t	pepper
40 oz	favorite spaghetti sauce (5 cups)
8 oz	lasagna noodles (or enough for 3 layers), uncooked
1 C	water
½ C	Parmesan cheese

In large bowl, mix ricotta, 1½ cup mozzarella, egg, spinach, salt, oregano, and pepper. In greased 13 x 9 x 2-inch baking dish, layer 1½ cup spaghetti sauce, ⅓ of noodles, and ½ of cheese-spinach mixture. Repeat layering. Top with remaining noodles, then remaining 2 cups of sauce. Sprinkle with remaining mozzarella cheese and Parmesan cheese. Pour water around edges. Cover tightly with foil. Bake at 350° for 1 hour 15 minutes (1 hour for pre-cooked noodles) or until bubbly. Let stand for 15 minutes before serving.

INSPIRATION: If using "no-boil" lasagna noodles, only add ½ cup water and bake for 1 hour. No-boil noodles have been pre-cooked which results in a thinner, more delicate noodle.

Pasta

Liz's Spaghetti with a Brown Sauce Baked in Foil

2 T	butter
2 T	olive oil
1	medium onion, finely chopped
2	cloves garlic
1 T	tomato paste
1 T	fresh thyme, finely chopped
2 C	good quality beef stock
8 oz	steak
8 oz	spaghetti
3 T	butter (optional for adding at the end)
½ C	Parmesan cheese, freshly grated

Prepare the sauce first. Sauce can be made early the day before to blend flavors. Sauté the onion in half the butter and oil, add garlic and simmer for 30 seconds. Mix in the tomato paste, thyme, and stock.

Cut steak into very small pieces. Sauté in the remaining butter and oil until browned on the outside and still pink inside. Cook the spaghetti in boiling water for five minutes and drain in colander. It will not be completely cooked through. Mix the spaghetti, meat mixture, and sauce together in a large foil baking pan. Add the Parmesan cheese and additional butter. Seal tightly with heavy-duty foil and bake at 350° for 15-20 minutes until the pasta is cooked.

INSPIRATION: This is a perfect dish to take to a potluck dinner or to a family whose Mom is under the weather. Sautéed mushrooms are a nice addition.

Pasta

MAIN

Roasted Asparagus with Balsamic Browned Butter

40	asparagus spears, trimmed (about 2 lbs)
	olive oil or cooking spray
¼ t	kosher salt
⅛ t	black pepper
2 T	butter
2 t	soy sauce
1 t	balsamic vinegar

Preheat oven to 400°. Arrange asparagus in a single layer on baking sheet, coat with cooking spray (or oil). Sprinkle with salt and pepper. Bake at 400° for 12 minutes or until tender. Melt butter in small skillet over medium heat. Cook for 3 minutes or until lightly browned, shaking pan occasionally. Remove from heat, stir in soy sauce and vinegar. Drizzle over asparagus, tossing well to coat. Serve immediately.

Accompaniments

Roasted Asparagus and Wild Mushroom Fricassee

SERVES
4

1 lb	medium asparagus, tough ends removed
2 t	olive oil
3 T	butter
1	large shallot, minced
12 oz	crimini and shiitake mushrooms, stems removed and sliced
½ C	dry white wine
1 T	fresh Italian parsley, minced

Preheat oven to 475°. Arrange asparagus on rimmed baking dish. Drizzle oil over and turn to coat. Sprinkle generously with salt and pepper. Roast until just tender, about 10 minutes.

Meanwhile, melt butter in large skillet over medium-high heat. Add shallot; sauté 1 minute. Add mushrooms; sauté until they begin to brown, about 5 minutes. Cover; cook until mushrooms are tender, about 3 minutes. Add wine; cook uncovered until wine is absorbed, about 2 minutes. Stir in parsley. Season to taste with salt and pepper.

Divide asparagus among 4 plates. Top each serving with mushrooms.

Accompaniments

Sautéed Artichoke Hearts

4	(14 oz) cans artichoke hearts, quartered
4	cups Italian style breadcrumbs
2 C	flour
3	eggs, beaten
	olive oil
1	lemon, quartered
	Italian parsley, chopped

Rinse and pat dry artichoke quarters. Toss them in the flour, and shake off excess. Coat with beaten egg, then coat with breadcrumbs. Set aside on paper towels until all the quarters are breaded.

Cover the bottom of a large, heavy skillet with olive oil ⅛-inch deep. Heat oil until a breaded artichoke bubbles around the edges when placed in oil. Test heat by carefully dipping in one end of an artichoke in the oil to see if it bubbles. Add artichokes to pan without overcrowding and fry until golden brown on both sides, turning once. Remove fried artichokes from oil, and place on paper towels to absorb excess oil before serving. Arrange golden brown artichokes on serving plate. Splash with a squeeze of lemon juice and garnish with chopped parsley.

Accompaniments

245

Mushroom and Artichoke Sauté

	juice from 1 large lemon
3 T	butter, melted
2 C	small fresh mushrooms
2	(14 oz) cans artichoke hearts, rinsed, drained, and quartered
1 T	dry sherry (optional)
	fresh parsley, chopped

Add lemon juice to melted butter and sauté mushrooms and artichoke hearts 12 minutes over medium heat. Add sherry. Continue to cook 2 more minutes. Toss with chopped parsley and serve.

Accompaniments

Baked Tomatoes and Artichokes

1	(14 oz) can Italian plum tomatoes (undrained)
4 oz	tomato sauce
1	(14 oz) can artichoke hearts, drained and quartered
½ C	onion, finely chopped
2 T	butter
2 T	flour
½ t	Dijon mustard
½ t	salt
½ t	dried oregano
⅛ t	dried thyme
¼ t	freshly ground pepper
⅔ C	Parmesan cheese, freshly grated

Preheat oven to 400°. Butter shallow baking dish. Melt butter in heavy large saucepan over low heat. Add flour, mustard, salt, oregano, thyme, and pepper and stir for 1 minute. Add tomatoes, sauce, artichokes, and onion and stir to combine thoroughly. Pour into prepared baking dish.

MAKE AHEAD: Cover and refrigerate up to one day ahead. Bring to room temperature before baking.

Sprinkle with Parmesan cheese. Bake until bubbling and top is golden brown, about 30 minutes. Serve hot.

Accompaniments

Brussels Sprouts to Crave

SERVES
4

1 lb	**Brussels sprouts**
	olive oil
	salt

Preheat oven to 350°. Peel outer leaves from Brussels sprouts and cut in halves. Place sprouts in a frying pan that can also go into the oven. Pour enough olive oil over to coat and sprinkle with salt. Sauté over medium-high heat until slightly browned, stirring occasionally. Take off heat and pour a little more oil over them. Place in preheated oven until tender and easy to pierce with a fork, about 5-10 minutes.

Accompaniments

Better Brussels Sprouts

3-3½ lbs	Brussels sprouts
2½ T	unsalted butter
2½ T	olive oil
8	cloves of garlic, coarsely chopped
1 C	chicken broth
	salt and freshly ground black pepper, to taste
2 T	unsalted butter, melted
2 T	parsley, chopped
	freshly squeezed lemon juice (optional)

Cut off stem ends from sprouts and remove any outer yellow leaves. Cut a small X in bottom of each sprout. Rinse in cold water, drain, and pat dry.

MAKE AHEAD: May be prepared up to this point one day ahead and stored in plastic bags in vegetable crisper.

Over low heat, melt 2½ tablespoons butter with oil in a large, heavy pot. Add garlic; cook for 2½-3½ minutes, or just until garlic starts to change color. Add sprouts; toss with butter mixture. Add chicken broth, salt, and pepper. Cover; cook over medium-low heat for 10-15 minutes, or until just tender. Stir once or twice. Do not overcook. Drain sprouts; return them to the pot.

Just before serving, toss with melted butter; adjust seasonings. Shake pot over medium-low flame to heat through. (Do not cook.) Toss with parsley, and lemon juice if desired. Serve immediately.

INSPIRATION: Stir in 1-2 teaspoons Dijon mustard before serving.

Accompaniments

Butter for Broccoli or Cauliflower

¼ C	butter, softened
1 T	Dijon
	grated rind from 1 lemon
	green onion or chives to taste

Prepare butter by combining all the ingredients, set aside. Steam broccoli or cauliflower pieces. Drain. Toss with seasoned butter.

Accompaniments

Gingered Spiced Carrots

1 T	olive oil
1½ C	onion, finely diced
2 T	fresh gingerroot, finely chopped
1 t	ground cinnamon
2 t	ground cumin
3 T	light brown sugar
2 lbs	carrots, sliced (about 6 C)
2 C	chicken stock
1 t	salt (omit if using salted chicken stock)
2 T	fresh dill

Heat the oil in a large skillet over medium heat. Add the onion and cook until it turns a golden color. Add the remaining ingredients, except for the salt and dill. Simmer until the carrots are tender but not mushy, about 15 minutes. Remove from the heat and allow to cool for 5 minutes. Stir in the salt and dill.

INSPIRATIONS: *These spicy carrots are a wonderful side dish for grilled meat or poultry. They are also delicious served cold as an appetizer or a salad. If tightly covered, they keep well in the refrigerator for at least 1 week, and the flavors get better every day.*

Accompaniments

251

Garden Carrot Mélange

2 C	baby carrots, halved
⅓ C	water
3 T	butter
¼ C	green and/or red pepper, chopped
1 C	medium yellow summer squash, cut in half lengthwise, then cut crosswise into ¼" slices
1 C	medium zucchini, cut in half lengthwise, then cut crosswise into ¼" slices
¼ t	salt
1 T	fresh basil leaves, chopped

Combine carrots and water in a 2-quart saucepan. Cover; cook over medium heat until carrots are just tender, 8-10 minutes. Drain. Add butter to carrots in pan. Add green pepper, squash, zucchini and salt. Cover; continue cooking, stirring occasionally, until squash is just tender, 6-8 minutes. Stir in basil.

Accompaniments

Carrots with Hazelnut Butter

½ C	hazelnuts (same as filberts)
3 lb	carrots
4 T	butter
3 T	lemon juice
½ t	salt
	freshly ground black pepper to taste

Place the hazelnuts in a small baking pan and toast in a preheated 350° oven for 10 minutes or until the skins start to crack. Cool slightly and rub together in a kitchen towel to remove as much skin as possible. Chop coarsely. Peel the carrots and slice on the diagonal into thin slices. Bring a large pan of water to a boil, add the carrots and cook until tender, about 5-7 minutes. Drain and pat dry.

MAKE AHEAD: The hazelnuts and carrots can be prepared a day ahead. Refrigerate the carrots and store the nuts in an airtight container. Bring both to room temperature before proceeding.

In a large pan melt the butter over medium heat. Add the lemon juice and stir to mix. Add the carrots, salt, and pepper; stir until carrots are heated through. Stir in nuts and serve.

Accompaniments

253

Corn Pudding

¼ C	onion, finely chopped
3 T	butter
3 T	flour
1 t	salt
1 t	pepper
1 T	sugar
1⅓ C	milk
2 oz	canned green chilies, drained and chopped
¼ C	fresh cilantro
2 T	red bell pepper, diced
dash	cayenne pepper
3 C	fresh or frozen corn, chopped
2	eggs

Preheat oven to 350°. Melt butter in large saucepan and sauté onion. Stir in flour, salt, sugar, green chilies, cilantro, red peppers and cayenne. Cook until bubbly. Add milk and cook until thickened. Stir in corn. Beat eggs and stir in. Pour into buttered 9 x 9-inch casserole pan and set in a 10 x 13-inch pan containing a 1-inch water bath of boiling water. Bake for 45 minutes to 1 hour.

Accompaniments

Mustard Green Beans and Cherry Tomatoes

1½ lbs	green beans, trimmed and cut into 1" pieces
3 T	balsamic vinegar
2 t	sugar
2 t	Dijon mustard
1 t	salt
¼ C	olive oil
¼ C	red onions, finely chopped
1 pt	cherry or grape tomatoes, halved
	freshly ground black pepper

In a large pot of boiling salted water, cook the beans until just crisp-tender, about 3 minutes. Drain and place in serving bowl. In medium bowl, whisk together vinegar, sugar, mustard, salt, and oil. Stir in red onions. Drizzle dressing over warm beans; top beans with tomatoes and sprinkle black pepper over all. Serve warm or at room temperature.

Accompaniments

255

Green Beans with Balsamic-Glazed Onions

2	(16 oz) bags frozen pearl onions, thawed
½ C	balsamic vinegar
2 T	butter
1 T	olive oil
2 t	fresh thyme, chopped (or 1 tsp dried thyme)
1½ t	freshly ground pepper
1 t	salt
2 lb	fresh green beans, trimmed
2 T	olive oil
1 T	Dijon mustard

Preheat oven to 400°. In a nonreactive saucepan, combine ¼ cup vinegar, butter, 1 tablespoon oil, thyme, 1 teaspoon pepper, and ½ teaspoon salt. Stir over medium heat until butter melts. Toss onions with vinegar mixture. Spread in a single layer on a baking sheet and roast for 35-40 minutes, stirring often, until evenly browned.

Meanwhile, in a large pot of boiling salted water, blanch green beans until just tender, about 4 minutes. Drain and rinse with cold water; drain and set aside.

In a large bowl, combine 2 tablespoons olive oil, Dijon mustard, remaining ¼ cup vinegar and ½ teaspoon each salt and pepper. Add beans and onions. Toss well. Transfer to a large casserole.

MAKE AHEAD: Recipe can be prepared a day ahead and refrigerated. Return to room temperature before proceeding.

In a preheated 350°oven, cover and bake beans and onions for 20 minutes or until heated through.

INSPIRATION: This is a great vegetable dish for a holiday buffet.

Green Beans and Parmesan with Garlic

1 lb	fresh green beans
1	large clove of garlic, crushed
	salt and pepper to taste
1 T	lemon juice
2 T	olive oil
¼ C	Parmesan cheese, grated

Trim and remove the strings from the beans. Combine the beans with enough water to cover in a saucepan. Bring to a boil; reduce heat. Simmer, covered, for 6-8 minutes or until tender-crisp; drain. Plunge the beans into ice water; drain. Sauté the garlic, salt, and pepper in the olive oil in a skillet. Add the lemon juice and beans and mix well. Sauté until heated through. Spoon onto a serving platter. Sprinkle with the cheese.

MAKE AHEAD: The beans may be blanched early in the day and stored in the refrigerator until just before preparation time.

INSPIRATIONS: You can sauté 1 cup fresh sliced mushrooms, or ⅓ cup chopped onions with the garlic for this dish.

Accompaniments

Gingered Green Bean Salad

SERVES
4-6

1 lb	green beans, trimmed and cut into 2" long pieces
⅓ C	almonds, blanched and sliced
1 T	dry mustard
2 t	water
1½ t	sugar
2 T	white or rice vinegar
1½ T	soy sauce
1 T	fresh ginger, finely shredded

In the top half of a vegetable steamer set over boiling water, steam beans for about 5 minutes, or until just tender. Rinse under cold water and pat dry.

In medium bowl, combine beans and almonds.

In small bowl, whisk together the mustard and water to make a paste. Stir in the vinegar, sugar, soy sauce, and ginger. Pour over bean mixture and toss to coat. Cover and refrigerate for at least 30 minutes before serving.

Accompaniments

Wild Mushroom Sauté

½ C	fresh Italian parsley leaves, packed
3	garlic cloves
3 T	extra-virgin olive oil
½ t	coarse sea salt
2 lbs	assorted fresh wild mushrooms (such as chanterelles, crimini, oyster, and stemmed shiitakes)
1 T	fresh lemon juice

Finely chop ½ cup parsley with 1 garlic clove; set parsley mixture aside. Finely chop remaining 2 garlic cloves. Whisk chopped garlic, 2 tablespoons oil and ½ teaspoon salt in large bowl to blend. Clean mushrooms and quarter the large mushrooms and halve the medium sized. Add the mushrooms to the garlic and oil mixture. Toss to coat.

Heat remaining 1 tablespoon olive oil in heavy large skillet over medium-high heat. Add mushroom mixture and sauté until mushrooms are brown and just tender, about 10 minutes. Remove skillet from heat. Mix in parsley mixture and lemon juice. Season to taste with salt and pepper. Serve.

Accompaniments

Sweet Onion Gratineé

4 C	sweet onions (Maui, Vidalia, or Walla Walla), sliced
2 T	olive oil
⅓ C	dry vermouth
2 T	cornstarch
1 T	butter
⅔ C	chicken broth
½ C	Gruyere cheese, grated

Sauté the onions in olive oil in a skillet until tender. Spoon into a 1½-quart baking dish. Toss ⅓ cup cheese into onions.

Combine the vermouth and cornstarch in a bowl, stirring until the cornstarch is dissolved. Heat 1 tablespoon butter in a saucepan until melted. Add the vermouth mixture, stirring until blended. Stir in the chicken broth. Cook until thickened, stirring constantly. Pour over the onions and gently work into onions. Sprinkle with the remaining cheese.

MAKE AHEAD: Casserole can be prepared, covered and refrigerated up to 1 day ahead. Bring to room temperature before baking.

Bake at 350° for 30 minutes, or until bubbly.

Accompaniments

Blue Cheese Vidalia Onions

2	very large Vidalia onions
6-8 oz	blue cheese, crumbled
2 T	butter, softened
2 t	Worcestershire sauce
½ t	dill weed
	freshly ground pepper

Preheat oven to 425°. Slice onions into ¼-½" thick slices and put in a 9 x 13-inch baking dish. Combine blue cheese, butter, Worcestershire, dill weed, and pepper. Spread over onions. Bake at 425° for 20 minutes or until brown and bubbly. Delicious served with our Herb Crusted New York Strip Roast (see Index).

Accompaniments

Roma Tomatoes with Crunchy Topping

2½ lb	ripe roma tomatoes
¼ C	extra-virgin olive oil
5	garlic cloves, 1 crushed and 4 minced
	salt and freshly ground pepper
¼ C	fresh basil, finely chopped
¼ C	flat-leaf parsley, finely chopped
1 C	fresh breadcrumbs made from Italian bread

Preheat the oven to 400°. Halve the tomatoes lengthwise. Working over a strainer in a bowl to catch the juices, discard the cores and seeds from the tomatoes. Set the tomatoes and juices aside. Rub the bottom and sides of a 14 x 10 x 2-inch ovenproof serving dish with 1 teaspoon of the olive oil, then with the crushed garlic clove. Reserve the garlic. Arrange the tomatoes cut side up in the dish. Sprinkle the reserved tomato juices and the minced garlic on top. Drizzle 2 tablespoons of the oil over the tomatoes and season with salt and pepper. Bake for 20 minutes. Sprinkle the basil on top and bake for 10 minutes longer. Turn off the heat but leave the dish in the oven for 20 minutes to allow the tomatoes to soften completely.

MAKE AHEAD: The tomatoes can be baked up to 6 hours ahead and set aside at room temperature. Briefly re-heat in a 400° oven before proceeding.

Meanwhile, in a heavy medium skillet combine the remaining olive oil, the reserved crushed garlic clove and the parsley and cook over moderate heat, stirring occasionally, for 5 minutes. Discard the crushed garlic. Add the breadcrumbs and cook, stirring, until golden brown and crisp, 7-8 minutes. Stir in ¼ teaspoon each of salt and pepper and set aside to cool.

MAKE AHEAD: The breadcrumbs can be made 1 day ahead; store in an airtight container at room temperature.

Sprinkle the breadcrumbs over the warm tomatoes and serve.

Layered Potatoes with Spinach and Tomato

¼ lb	pancetta or bacon, diced
1	medium onion, thinly sliced
1	(10 oz) pkg frozen spinach, defrosted and well-drained
1½ C	2% milk
1	egg, beaten
2 t	salt
⅛ t	pepper
½ t	oregano
2	cloves garlic, crushed
4 lbs	russet potatoes (4 large), peeled and sliced ⅛"
1	(28 oz) can plum tomatoes, drained and chopped
4 oz	Gruyere or provolone, grated and divided

Preheat oven to 450°. Over medium heat, combine the pancetta or bacon and onion. If necessary, add some oil and cook until the onion is golden brown, about 10 minutes. Remove from heat, mix in the well-drained spinach and set aside. Meanwhile, combine milk, egg, salt, pepper, oregano, and garlic.

Spray a 9 x 13-inch baking dish with oil. Divide the sliced potatoes in thirds. Layer the first third overlapping slightly in dish. Spread tomatoes evenly over top and cover with ⅓ of milk mixture. Layer the next third of potatoes and then the spinach mixture, spreading evenly. Sprinkle with half of the cheese. Cover with another third of the milk mixture. Finish with the last third of potatoes and pour the remaining milk mixture evenly over the dish.

Cover with foil and bake 45 minutes. Remove foil, sprinkle with remaining cheese and bake another 10 minutes or until the cheese begins to brown. Remove from oven and let rest, covered, for 10 minutes. To serve, cut into squares.

Accompaniments

Potato Gratin

1	clove garlic, halved
	cooking spray
1 C	onion, chopped
6	medium-size red potatoes, peeled and cut into ⅛" slices (about 2½ lbs)
¼ t	salt
¼ t	freshly ground pepper
¾ C	extra-sharp Cheddar cheese (3 oz), shredded
¼ C	fresh Romano cheese, grated
1 C	chicken broth
1 C	evaporated skimmed milk

Preheat oven to 425°. Rub a shallow 3-quart dish with cut sides of garlic halves; discard garlic. Coat dish with cooking spray. Coat a small nonstick skillet with cooking spray; place over medium heat until hot. Add onion and sauté 5 minutes or until tender; set aside. Arrange ⅓ of potato slices in prepared dish, and sprinkle with half of salt and half of pepper. Top with half of sautéed onion and half of Cheddar and Romano cheese. Repeat layers, ending with the remaining potato slices. Bring milk to a boil over low heat in a small saucepan; pour over potato mixture. Bake, uncovered, for 50 minutes or until tender. Let stand 5 minutes before serving.

Accompaniments

Horseradish Scalloped Potatoes

3½ C	heavy cream
2	garlic cloves, minced
1¾ t	salt
½ t	freshly ground pepper
4 T	prepared horseradish, drained
2¾ lb	Idaho potatoes, peeled and sliced thinly
1½	large Granny Smith apples, peeled, halved, cored, and thinly sliced
¼ C	Parmesan cheese, freshly grated

Preheat oven to 400°. In a bowl, combine the heavy cream, garlic, salt, and pepper. Gradually stir in the horseradish, tasting for strength. In a 9 x 13-inch glass baking dish, place 3 layers of potatoes, then layer the apples and top with remaining layer of potatoes. Pour the seasoned cream over the potatoes.

MAKE AHEAD: The potatoes can be prepared to this point up to 2 hours ahead. Do not refrigerate.

Bake in the upper third of the oven for 30 minutes, or until bubbling. Sprinkle the Parmesan cheese over the top and bake for about 15 minutes longer, or until the potatoes are tender and the top is nicely browned. Cover the gratin with foil and let stand in a warm place for 10-30 minutes before serving. Cut the gratin into 12 squares.

INSPIRATION: This gratin is a wonderful accompaniment to serve with beef.

Accompaniments

Holiday Potatoes

3 lb	potatoes, some red and white, cut and cubed (must be peeled)
¼ C	onion, chopped
8 oz	cream cheese, cubed
¼ C	butter, softened
½ C	milk
2	eggs, beaten
1 t	salt
	fresh chives, chopped

Cook potatoes and onion in boiling water until tender, drain. Add cream cheese, butter, and milk. Beat until combined with a mixer and add eggs and salt. Continue to mix until potatoes are fluffy. Pour into greased casserole dish, top with chopped fresh chives and bake 45 minutes at 350°.

MAKE AHEAD: This dish can be prepared and refrigerated overnight. Bring to room temperature before baking.

Accompaniments

Golden Mashed Potato and Shallot Casserole

1½ T	butter
3-4	medium shallots (4½ oz), thinly sliced
1½ t	sugar
3½ lb	Yukon Gold potatoes, peeled and cut into 2" pieces (8 cups) *Although Russet or Red potatoes can be substituted; the Yukon Gold potatoes give a golden color to the casserole.
4 oz	light cream cheese
¾ C	light sour cream
½ t	salt
½ t	freshly ground black pepper

Preheat oven to 400°. Spray a 2½-quart casserole with cooking spray. Melt the butter in a skillet over medium heat. Add the shallots, stir to coat with butter, and then sprinkle with sugar. Cook until the shallots are golden, stirring occasionally, about 10 minutes.

Put the potatoes in a large saucepan, cover with salted water, and bring to a boil. Reduce the heat to low and simmer until tender, about 20-25 minutes. While the potatoes are cooking, beat together cream cheese, sour cream, salt, and pepper. Stir in the cooked shallots.

Drain potatoes and mash with potato masher or ricer. Add the cream cheese mixture and mix until fluffy and smooth. Do not over mix as potatoes will become gummy. Spread the potato mixture evenly in the prepared casserole dish. Cover and bake in the preheated oven for 25 minutes. Remove the cover and continue to bake for 10 more minutes.

MAKE AHEAD: This casserole can be prepared and refrigerated for up to 24 hours. Bring the casserole to room temperature before baking.

INSPIRATION: Leftovers make delicious potato pancakes. Form into patties and lightly sauté. Top with sour cream and chives.

Accompaniments

267

Roasted Potatoes with Lime and Basil

1½ lb	small new potatoes, cut into ¾" pieces
3 T	olive oil
½ C	packed fresh basil leaves, chopped fine
1 T	fresh lime juice

Preheat oven to 450°. In a baking dish or sheet pan large enough to hold potatoes in one layer, toss them with oil and salt and pepper to taste. Roast potatoes in middle of oven until tender about 20-25 minutes. In a bowl, toss potatoes with lime juice and basil.

Accompaniments

Sweet Potato, Onion, and Bacon Compote

SERVES
4-6

4	slices premium smoked bacon, chopped
1-2 T	unsalted butter
½	medium onion, chopped fine
1 lb	mushrooms, mix of white and wild, sliced
¼ C	chicken stock
1 T	cider vinegar
1 T	dark brown sugar
1½ t	unsulphured dark molasses
½ t	Worcestershire sauce
½ t	fresh ground black pepper
¼ t	dried thyme
¼ t	pepper flakes or 2 T poblano peppers, chopped
⅛ t	powdered ginger or 1 t fresh grated ginger
	salt to taste
¾ lb	sweet potato, peeled and diced in bite-size pieces
1 dz	pearl onions, blanched and peeled (or frozen)

In a large skillet, fry the bacon over medium heat until it is browned and crisp. Remove and drain the bacon, set aside. Melt butter in the drippings. Add the onion and the mushrooms, and sauté them over medium heat until they are softened, 2-3 minutes.

Add to the skillet the stock, vinegar, brown sugar, molasses, Worcestershire sauce, pepper, thyme, pepper flakes, ginger, and a touch of salt, and mix well. Stir in the sweet potatoes, and simmer over medium heat 2-3 minutes. Add the pearl onions, cover the pan, and continue to cook another 7-10 minutes, until both the potatoes and onions are tender. The dish can be made ahead and covered to this point 1 hour in advance of your meal.

Uncover the pan, and cook another couple of minutes, stirring continually, until the sauce reduces to a glaze. Sprinkle in the reserved bacon, and stir to mix. Taste, add a little more salt if you like, and serve.

Accompaniments

Julienned Sweet Potato and Green Beans

4	sweet potatoes, julienned in ¼" wide strips
5 oz	green beans, trimmed
	salt and pepper
1 t	honey
1C	almonds, sliced or slivered, and toasted

Preheat oven to 350°. Bake sweet potatoes and green beans in oven for 20 minutes or until tender. Toss with honey and almonds. Bake for another 5 minutes. Serve.

Accompaniments

Zesty Orange Sweet Potato and Squash

1½ lbs	butternut squash (1 small)
¾ lb	sweet potatoes (2 small)
1½ t	freshly grated orange zest
1½ t	fresh orange juice
	salt to taste

Preheat oven to 375°. Prick squash and sweet potatoes with a fork; roast on a baking sheet for 50-60 minutes, or until tender (or microwave). Cut vegetables in half; remove and discard squash seeds. When cool enough to handle, scoop flesh into a bowl. Add orange zest and juice. Mash until smooth. Season with salt and butter if desired. Keep warm.

INSPIRATION: This is delicious served with our Chicken with Pear and Mushroom Sauce (see Index).

Accompaniments

271

Spinach Casserole

6	slices lean bacon
6	(10 oz) pkgs frozen chopped spinach
1	stick butter, softened
12 oz	cream cheese, softened
½ C	Romano and/or Parmesan cheese, grated
3 T	cheese, grated

Cook bacon until crisp. Drain on paper towels and crumble into small pieces. Cook spinach according to directions on package. Drain well.

Combine butter and cream cheese. Add ½ cup cheese and spinach. Mix well. Put into buttered shallow, oven-proof casserole dish. Top with bacon and 3 tablespoons grated cheese.

Heat in oven at 350°, until hot and bubbly.

Accompaniments

Spinach Stuffed Tomatoes

1	(10 oz) bag fresh spinach
4	large tomatoes
3	green onions, chopped
½ C	sour cream
¾ C	Parmesan cheese
2	dashes cayenne pepper
1½ T	breadcrumbs
1 T	butter
	salt and pepper to taste

Cut tops of tomatoes, scoop out center, leaving sides firm. Be careful not to puncture sides. Salt and drain upside down for 15 minutes.

Steam spinach 1-2 minutes, drain excess water in strainer and chop.

Preheat oven to 350°. Cut green onions and sauté in 1 tablespoon butter. Add spinach, sour cream, Parmesan cheese, cayenne, salt and pepper to taste. Add 1 tablespoon of breadcrumbs. Stuff tomatoes and top with remaining cheese and ½ tablespoon breadcrumbs. Bake approximately 20 minutes.

Accompaniments

273

Use up the Zucchini

7-8	medium zucchini, sliced ¼"
2 t	salt
8	slices bacon, diced
1	large onion, chopped
1	large clove of garlic, minced
4	slices of bread, crumbled
2 C	mozzarella cheese, shredded
1 t	Italian seasoning
	black pepper
1	(15oz) can tomato sauce
¼ C	grated Parmesan

Preheat oven 425°. Lightly oil 13 x 9-inch oven proof dish. Cook zucchini in 2 cups boiling water and 1 teaspoon salt for 3-5 minutes. Drain. Cook bacon until crisp. Drain and put in a bowl. Add onion and garlic to bacon fat. Sauté 5-6 minutes. Drain. Add to bowl. Add everything except Parmesan cheese to the bowl and toss. Spoon into baking dish. Sprinkle with Parmesan cheese and bake 20 minutes or until bubbly.

Accompaniments

Zucchini Bake

SERVES
6

8-10	zucchini
1 T	butter
½ C	chopped onion
1 C	Cheddar cheese, grated
½ C	Gruyere cheese, grated
1 C	sour cream
½ t	paprika
1 C	breadcrumbs
	grated Parmesan cheese

Preheat oven to 350°. Boil zucchini 8-10 minutes. Cut off ends and halve lengthwise. Arrange in shallow buttered casserole dish. Sauté onion in butter. Add both cheeses and sour cream to onions and mix well. Spread onion cheese mixture over zucchini. Top with crumbs mixed with Parmesan cheese. Bake for 45 minutes.

Accompaniments

275

BBQ Black Beans with Rum

1 C	onions, diced
4	garlic cloves, finely chopped
2	jalapeño peppers, seeded and chopped
1 T	olive oil
½ C	ketchup
¼ C	molasses
½ C	dark rum
¼ C	prepared mustard
2 T	brown sugar
2 T	Worcestershire sauce
1 T	hot sauce
½ t	ground ginger
3	(15 oz) cans black beans, drained

Heat tablespoon of olive oil in large pan. Add onion, garlic, and jalapeños to pan. Cook 5 minutes or until onion is tender. Stir in ketchup and remaining ingredients except beans. Bring to a boil. Reduce heat and simmer 5 minutes, stirring occasionally. Stir in the beans, and simmer for 1 hour over very low heat stirring occasionally. Watch carefully so beans don't stick to the pan.

INSPIRATION: Add 5 ounces of cooked, diced chorizo or other smoked sausage to this dish when you add the beans.

Accompaniments

Black Bean Cakes

2	(15 oz) cans black beans
6 T	salsa
6 T	sweet or green onion, finely diced
¾ C	red bell pepper, finely diced
3 T	fresh cilantro, chopped
1½ C	breadcrumbs
¼ C	poblano pepper, mild flavor or 1 T jalapeño, diced
1	large garlic clove, minced
2 t	chipotle sauce or to taste or ½ t hot sauce
1½ T	lemon juice
	salt and pepper to taste

Tortilla Chip Breading

1½ C	tortilla chips, crushed (baked variety works well)
1 t	cumin

Place beans in a colander and rinse in cold water. Drain well, for at least 10 minutes. Add drained beans and all the other ingredients except for tortilla chip breading into a mixing bowl. Blend well, mashing some of the beans to form a thick mixture. Form into 6 patties and roll in tortilla breading. At this point you can cover and refrigerate until ready to heat. Heat skillet, sauté in just enough oil to brown cakes and heat through. Serve with fresh tomato salsa.

INSPIRATION: These can be served as a vegetarian entrée. They are especially good served with our Caesar Salad with Southwestern Dressing (see Index).

Accompaniments

Hearty Mushroom Risotto

3	large shallots, chopped
1½ T	olive oil
8 oz	portabello, crimini, and/or shiitake mushrooms without stems, sliced
1 C	white wine
12 oz	button mushrooms, sliced
1½ C	uncooked Arborio rice
3-4 C	chicken stock
2 T	Parmesan cheese
2 T	butter
¼ C	white wine
¼ t	salt
½ t	pepper

Sauté the shallots in ½ tablespoon olive oil in a nonstick skillet over medium heat for 1-2 minutes or until tender. Stir in portabella mushrooms and ½ cup of wine. Cook for 4 minutes. Add remaining ½ cup wine and button mushrooms. Pour into large saucepan. Sauté rice in 1 tablespoon olive oil in same skillet for 2 minutes, stirring constantly. Stir into mushroom mixture.

Meanwhile, heat chicken stock in saucepan to just below simmering point, turn off heat but cover to keep warm. Stir ½ cup of stock into rice and mushroom mixture. Cook until most of liquid has been absorbed, stirring constantly. Add remaining stock, ½ cup at a time. Cook until stock is absorbed after each addition. Cook until rice is tender and mixture is creamy. Stir in the cheese, butter, ¼ cup wine, salt, and pepper. Cover until ready to serve. Garnish with additional Parmesan cheese.

Accompaniments

Spring Risotto with Asparagus

⅓ C	onion, finely chopped
1 T	butter
1 T	olive oil
1⅓ C	Arborio rice
2	(14 oz) cans reduced sodium chicken broth
10-12	stalks asparagus, cut into 1" pieces
¼ C	dry white wine
⅓ C	imported Parmesan cheese, finely shredded
1½ oz	prosciutto or ham, thinly sliced and cut into thin strips

In a large saucepan cook onion in butter and olive oil over medium heat until tender. Add uncooked rice. Cook and stir about 1 minute. In another saucepan bring broth to boiling; reduce heat and simmer, covered.

Slowly add 1 cup of hot broth to the rice mixture, stirring constantly. Cook and stir until liquid is absorbed. Continue adding broth, ½ cup at a time, stirring constantly until the broth has been absorbed. Repeat with the wine.

The rice should be creamy and barely firm; it should take 30 minutes to get to this point. Stir in the ⅓ cup cheese and remove from heat. Stir in prosciutto and serve.

INSPIRATION: Serve this risotto as a main dish entrée along with a green salad.

Accompaniments

279

Green Chili Rice

1 C	onion, chopped
1 T	butter
4 C	cooked rice
12 oz	1% cottage cheese
16 oz	light sour cream
2 C	Cheddar cheese, grated
2	(4 oz) cans green chilies, drained and chopped
¾ t	salt
⅛ t	pepper
¼ C	parsley
	cayenne pepper, about 4 shakes

Sauté onion in butter. Combine cottage cheese, sour cream, 1 cup of Cheddar cheese, chilies, sautéed onions, parsley, cayenne pepper, salt, and pepper and mix thoroughly. Add the cheese mixture to the rice and gently mix together. Pour rice mixture in lightly greased 9x13-inch pan.

MAKE AHEAD: At this point, the casserole can be covered and refrigerated up to 24 hours. Bring rice to room temperature before baking.

Bake covered at 350° for 45 minutes, remove from oven and add the remaining cup of cheese across the top. Return to oven uncovered until cheese is browned and bubbly, about 10 minutes.

Accompaniments

Spinach and Feta Rice

1 T	olive oil
1	large onion, chopped
1	large garlic clove, minced
¾ C	long-grain white rice
2 C	canned beef broth or chicken broth
¼ C	dry white wine
2 C	fresh spinach, chopped
½ C	tomatoes, seeded and chopped
1 C	feta cheese, crumbled

Heat oil in heavy large pot over medium-high heat. Add onion and garlic and sauté until onion is tender, about 6 minutes. Add rice and stir until rice is translucent, about 2 minutes. Add broth and wine and bring to boil. Reduce heat to low; cover and cook until rice is almost tender, about 15 minutes. Mix in spinach. Cover and cook until rice and spinach are tender and all liquid is absorbed, about 8 minutes longer. Mix in tomatoes and cheese. Season with salt and pepper and serve.

INSPIRATION: This rice is a delicious accompaniment to our Greek-Style Chicken and Mushrooms (see Index).

Accompaniments

281

Five Spice Rice

1 t	sesame oil
¾ C	carrots, diced
½ C	onion, diced
2	cloves garlic, minced
2	(10½ oz) cans chicken broth
½ t	Chinese five-spice
¼ t	salt
¼ t	pepper
1¼ C	long-grain rice, uncooked

Heat oil in pan and add onion, carrot, and garlic; sauté until tender. Add broth, Chinese five-spice, salt and pepper, bring to a boil. Stir in rice and return to boil. Cover and reduce heat and cook 20 minutes.

Accompaniments

Spirited Wild Rice

1 C	golden raisins
½ C	dry sherry
1 C	wild rice
	water to cook the wild rice
2¼ C	chicken stock
2 T	butter
1 C	brown rice
1 C	slivered almonds, toasted
½ C	fresh parsley, chopped
	salt and pepper to taste

Combine the raisins and sherry. Heat in a small pan or microwave for a few minutes and set aside. Cook the wild rice in water following the directions on the package.

Combine the brown rice, 2 tablespoons butter, and the stock in a pan. Bring to a boil, cover, and cook for about 45 minutes until done. Let stand off the heat for 5 minutes to finish cooking.

Combine the two types of rice, nuts, raisins, parsley, and season to taste.

Accompaniments

283

Turkish Pilaf

1	(4 oz) can mushrooms and juice
8-10	spring onions, chopped
¼ lb	butter
2 t	oregano
2 C	long-grain rice
3	(10 oz) cans consommé
2	(10 oz) cans water
1	chicken bouillon cube

Sauté mushrooms, juice, spring onions, butter, and oregano. Add long-grain rice and consommé, water, and bouillon. Bring to a boil. Simmer uncovered for 35 minutes or until all liquid is absorbed.

Bulghur Pilaf

2 T	onion, finely chopped
2 T	green pepper, chopped
2 T	butter
2 C	chicken broth
1 C	uncooked bulghur wheat
1	(3 oz) can sliced mushrooms, drained
½ t	salt
dash	pepper

Cook and stir onion and green pepper in butter in 10-inch skillet until onion is tender. Stir in remaining ingredients. Cover and heat to boiling. Reduce heat and simmer 15 minutes or until tender.

Accompaniments

Couscous with Cranberries and Nuts

1 C	couscous
1¼ C	water
1 T	butter or olive oil
¼ C	fresh orange juice
½ C	dried cranberries
½ C	pecans or walnuts, chopped
1 T	grated orange rind
¼ t	ground cumin
⅛ t	cinnamon
2 T	chopped fresh parsley and/or chives
	salt and pepper to taste

Bring water and butter to a boil in a medium saucepan. Remove from heat and stir in couscous. Cover and let stand 5 minutes. Combine cranberries and orange juice in a small dish. Cover and heat in microwave until cranberries are hot enough to absorb the liquid. Set aside. Fluff couscous with a fork and add the cranberries, nuts, rind and seasonings. Add salt and pepper to taste. Add additional orange juice if needed.

MAKE AHEAD: This dish can be prepared up to one day ahead and re-heated in a microwave before serving.

Accompaniments

Creamy Stone-ground Grits

1 T	butter
2 T	onion
1⅔ C	chicken stock
2 T	half & half or milk
½ C	stone-ground white or yellow grits (not quick-cook)
2 T	low-fat or regular cream cheese
¼ t	salt
	fresh ground white pepper
¼ C	Parmesan cheese
¼ C	green onion tops

Sauté onion in butter. Add chicken stock and half & half; bring to a boil. Whisk in the grits. Reduce heat, cover, and simmer for 15 minutes. Stir in cream cheese, salt, and pepper. Continue to simmer 1-2 minutes longer until grits are creamy. Stir in Parmesan cheese and green onions. Cover and keep warm.

Accompaniments

287

Bread Pudding with Sweet Corn

1	leek, white and light green part only, cut into semicircles
6	ears fresh corn or 3 C frozen
6 C	milk, warmed
¼ t	freshly grated nutmeg
1 T	olive oil
2 t	salt
½ t	pepper
2-3	yellow summer squash, ¼" slices (3 cups)
3 T	fresh sage, finely chopped or 1 t dried
5	large eggs plus 4 large egg yolks
1 lb	loaf Italian style semolina bread (dense bread) cut into 1" cubes
2 C	Romano cheese, freshly grated
1 T	unsalted butter

Place leeks in a large bowl of cold water and let sit for about 10 minutes to rid them of dirt and sand. Drain in a colander and set aside. Use a sharp knife to remove kernels from ears of corn and set aside. Place corncobs in a medium saucepan. Add milk and nutmeg and bring to a simmer over medium-high heat. Remove from heat, cover, and steep for 30 minutes. Remove cobs, scrap with a knife to extract as much flavor as possible. Discard cobs and set milk aside.

Preheat oven to 350°. Heat olive oil in a large skillet over medium-low heat. Add leeks, 1 teaspoon salt, and ¼ teaspoon pepper. Cook stirring frequently until translucent, about 10 minutes. Add squash and 2 tablespoons sage, cook until just tender, 8 minutes more. Add corn and cook 3 minutes more. Remove from heat and set aside.

In a large bowl, whisk together the warm milk, eggs, yolks, and remaining teaspoon salt and ¼ teaspoon pepper. Add bread cubes and let stand until bread is soaked through to center about 10 minutes. Add vegetables and 1 cup of cheese and mix well. Transfer into a buttered 11 x 13-inch dish. Sprinkle with remaining sage and cheese. Bake until pudding is puffed, set, and golden brown, 45 minutes to 1 hour or up to 1½ hours if using a smaller dish. Serve immediately or at room temperature.

Corn and Hazelnut Spoon Bread

SERVES
6

¼ C	hazelnuts (same as filberts)
1 C	yellow cornmeal
2 C	boiling water
2 C	fresh corn (about 4 ears), divided (or frozen, thawed)
1¼ C	low-fat milk
2 T	butter, melted
1 T	sugar
½ t	salt
2	egg yolks
2 t	baking powder
4	egg whites, at room temperature

Preheat oven to 350°. Place hazelnuts on a small baking sheet. Bake for 10-15 minutes, stirring once until skins start to crack. Cool slightly and rub together in a kitchen towel to remove as much skin as possible. Process nuts in food processor until finely ground. Set aside.

Blanch corn for 3 minutes in boiling water or place in microwave with husks on and cook for about 5 minutes for 2 ears. Repeat with other ears of corn. Cut off cob.

Place cornmeal in a large bowl. Gradually add 2 cups boiling water, stirring with a whisk until blended. Let stand 10 minutes. Place 1 cup of corn, milk, butter, sugar, salt, and egg yolks in a food processor, process until smooth. Add this to cornmeal mixture. Stir in hazelnuts, remaining 1 cup of corn, and baking powder; set aside. Beat egg whites just until stiff peaks form. Gently fold egg whites into cornmeal mixture. Spoon into a greased 2-quart round baking dish (like a soufflé dish). Bake at 350° for 40-50 minutes or until puffy, lightly browned and set.

This dish is very similar to a soufflé, so it may fall after it is removed from the oven. This will not affect the taste at all!

Swiss Alps Rice Pudding

SERVES
8-10

1 C	long-grain white rice, uncooked
4 T	butter or margarine
⅛ t	salt
1 qt	milk
¾ C	sugar, divided
2 t	vanilla extract
1 C	Swiss cheese (4 oz), grated
4	eggs
2	tart cooking apples, peeled, cored, and thinly sliced
1 t	ground cinnamon

In 2-quart saucepan, combine rice, butter, milk, ½ cup sugar and salt. Bring just to a boiling point. Reduce heat; cover and simmer 20 minutes or until rice is tender. (There will still be quite a bit of milk remaining in the pan.) Remove from heat; stir in vanilla and cheese; set aside

Preheat oven to 350°. Beat eggs in small mixing bowl. Slowly add 1 cup of hot rice mixture, beating constantly. Return contents of small bowl to saucepan; stir to thoroughly combine with rice mixture in saucepan. Pour into greased 9-inch square baking pan. Place apple slices on rice mixture. Stir cinnamon into remaining ¼ cup sugar; sprinkle mixture evenly over top of pudding. Bake in oven for 30 minutes.

INSPIRATION: This unusual dish is actually very good served with pork or ham.

Accompaniments

Swiss Chard Strudel

1	bunch Swiss chard (about 10 oz)
4 T	olive oil, divided
1	small Vidalia onion, chopped
½ t	salt
	freshly ground pepper to taste
¼ t	Creole seasoning
½ C	Jarlsberg cheese, shredded
3 T	dried breadcrumbs, unseasoned and fine, divided
2 T	Parmesan cheese, grated
3 T	unsalted butter, melted
6	sheets phyllo dough, thawed if frozen

Preheat oven to 375°. Rinse and drain chard. Remove the stems, trim and discard woody bottoms; chop the stems, and set aside. Coarsely chop the leaves. Heat 2 tablespoons of the oil in a skillet over low heat. Add the onion and sauté until tender, about 5 minutes. Stir in the chard stems and cook for 3 minutes. Add the chard leaves, and cook for 3 minutes more. Drain off excess liquid and transfer the mixture to a bowl. Season with salt, pepper, and Creole seasoning. Stir in the Jarlsberg, 1 tablespoon of the crumbs, and the Parmesan. Check seasoning and adjust to taste. Set aside.

Stir the butter and the remaining 2 tablespoons of olive oil together in a small bowl. Open 1 sheet of phyllo on a work surface. Brush it with some of the butter and oil mixture. Sprinkle with 1 teaspoon of the crumbs. Top with 4 more sheets of phyllo, brushing each with butter and oil and sprinkling each with crumbs. Top with remaining sheet, and brush it with butter and oil. Spoon the filling along one short end of the phyllo, leaving about 1½-inches empty on each side. Fold the long sides in, overlapping the filling by 1½-inches to enclose the ends of the filling. Roll the phyllo and filling over onto itself to form a strudel roll. Place it on a baking sheet seam side down and brush the top with any remaining butter and oil. Bake until deep golden, about 25 minutes. Let the strudel stand for 5 minutes before slicing and serving.

Accompaniments

291

Cranberry Apple Casserole

5-6	medium apples, (4-5 cups) Granny Smith, Gala, or Winesap, peeled and diced
1 C	cranberries
¾ C	sugar
1	stick butter
1 C	oatmeal
⅓ C	flour
½ C	brown sugar
½ C	nuts, pecans or walnuts, chopped

Preheat oven to 350°. Place apples and cranberries in a 9 x 13-inch casserole dish. Mix in sugar. In a sauce pan, melt the butter. Add oatmeal, flour, brown sugar, and nuts. Mix together and spread on top of apples and cranberries. Bake covered for 1 hour.

INSPIRATIONS: This is excellent served with meats, but can also be served as a dessert.

Accompaniments

POST

desserts

everything else

Lemon Rosemary Tea Cake

Cake

2 C	flour
1½ t	baking powder
¼ t	salt
2 t	lemon zest, grated
2 t	dried rosemary, minced or 4 tsp fresh, stripped from stems and minced
⅓ C	light olive oil
1 C	sugar
2	large eggs
¾ C	low-fat buttermilk

Glaze

2-3 T	fresh lemon juice
¾ C	confectioners sugar, sifted

Preheat oven to 325°. Lightly oil 9 x 5-inch loaf pan. Combine flour, baking powder, lemon zest, rosemary, and salt in medium bowl and stir to blend. In a large bowl beat the oil and sugar until well blended. Add the eggs one at a time, beating well after each addition until mixture is a pale yellow. Add ⅓ of flour mixture to egg mixture. Add half of buttermilk, stir to blend. Add remaining buttermilk, stir to blend. Add ⅓ more of flour mixture, stir to blend. Add remaining flour and stir to blend. Spread mixture in prepared pan. Bake until bread is golden and sides begin to pull away from pan, 50-55 minutes.

To prepare glaze, in a medium bowl, stir confectioners sugar and lemon juice until smooth; spread on the warm loaf. Cool thoroughly. Use a knife to loosen sides of bread from pan and turn out. Serve in slices.

Desserts

Kentucky Butter Cake

Cake

3 C	flour
2 C	sugar
1 t	salt
1 t	baking powder
½ t	baking soda
1 C	buttermilk
1 C	butter, softened
2 t	vanilla or rum extract
4	eggs

Butter Sauce

¾ C	sugar
⅓ C	butter
3 T	water
1-2 t	vanilla or rum extract
	powdered sugar for garnish

Preheat oven to 325°. Generously grease and lightly flour 12-cup Bundt pan or 10-inch tube pan. In large bowl, blend all cake ingredients at low speed until moistened. Beat 3 minutes at medium speed. Pour batter into greased and floured pan. Bake for 55-70 minutes until toothpick inserted in center comes out clean.

In small sauce pan over low heat, combine all sauce ingredients, stirring occasionally until butter melts. DO NOT BOIL. Using long-tined fork, pierce cake 10-12 times. Slowly pour hot sauce over cake. Remove cake from pan immediately after sauce has been absorbed, 5-10 minutes.

Just before serving sprinkle with powdered sugar. Serve with whipped cream, if desired.

Desserts

German Apple Cake

5	Granny Smith apples, peeled, ¼" slices
5 T	sugar
4 t	cinnamon
3 C	flour
1 T	baking powder
½ t	salt
2¼ C	sugar
4	eggs
⅓ C	orange juice
1 C	vegetable oil
2 t	vanilla

Preheat oven to 350°. Mix 5 tablespoons of sugar and cinnamon in small bowl. Toss into apples and set aside.

Sift flour, baking powder, and salt together. Mix sugar, eggs, orange juice, oil and vanilla in large bowl. Add flour mixture; mix well.

Spoon batter and apple mixture alternately into lightly greased tube pan until all ingredients are used, beginning with batter and ending with apple mixture. Bake for 1¼-1½ hours. Cool for 20 minutes. Remove from pan. If desired, flip so apples are on the top.

INSPIRATION: This moist, dense cake may be served as a breakfast cake. You can also add ¾ cup chopped walnuts or pecans to the apple mixture.

Desserts

Chocolate Upside Down Cake

1 C	flour
¾ C	sugar
2 T	cocoa
2 t	baking powder
¼ t	salt
½ C	milk
4 T	shortening
1 t	vanilla
½ C	pecans, walnuts, or almonds, chopped
½ C	white sugar
½ C	brown sugar
2 T	cocoa

Preheat oven to 350°. Sift together flour, ¾ cup sugar, cocoa, baking powder, and salt. Then add ½ cup milk and beat well. Add 4 tablespoons of shortening and 1 teaspoon vanilla and beat until fluffy. Mix in ½ cup nuts and pour into well greased and floured pan (about 7 x 10-inch).

Combine ½ cup white sugar, ½ cup brown sugar, and 2 tablespoons cocoa in separate bowl. Mix well and sprinkle over top cake batter. Pour 1 cup of cold water on top, and then bake for 30 minutes. Leave the cake in the pan.

To serve, cut into squares, then with a spatula lift and turn each piece upside down. The icing will be on top.

INSPIRATION: *This cake is delicious served warm with vanilla or mint chocolate chip ice cream.*

Chocolate Sour Cream Pound Cake

Cake

1 C	butter, softened
2 C	sugar
2	eggs
2 oz	unsweetened chocolate, melted
2 t	vanilla
2 t	baking soda
2½ C	flour
¼ t	salt
8 oz	sour cream (do not use reduced fat)
1 C	boiling water

Frosting

½ C	butter, softened
3 C	powdered sugar
2 oz	unsweetened chocolate, melted
¼ C	hot water
½ t	vanilla

Preheat oven to 325°. Have all ingredients at room temperature. Cream butter and sugar. Add eggs, melted chocolate, and vanilla to creamed mixture. Mix baking soda, flour, and salt. Add to chocolate, alternating with sour cream. Gradually add boiling water to mixture, blending well. Pour into greased and floured tube pan. Bake for 50-55 minutes or until done. Cool in pan for 20 minutes before removing from pan. Cool cake completely before frosting.

To prepare frosting, cream butter. Add sugar, chocolate, and water. Beat until creamy and smooth. Spread on cooled cake.

INSPIRATION: This rich moist cake is even better the second and third day.

Desserts

Sticky Toffee Pudding Cake

Sauce

4 C	heavy cream
2 C	dark brown sugar, packed
½ C	unsalted butter

Cake

2½ C	flour
2 t	baking powder
1½ C	water
1¼ C	dates, chopped
2 t	baking soda
1 C	unsalted butter, softened
⅔ C	sugar
4	large eggs
2 t	vanilla

For sauce: Bring cream, brown sugar, and butter to a boil in a heavy pan, stirring often. Reduce heat and simmer about 6 minutes to reduce to 3½ cups, stirring occasionally. Set aside.

For cake: Preheat oven to 350°. Butter a 12-cup bundt pan. Whisk flour and baking powder in medium bowl. Combine 1½ cups of water, dates, and baking soda in a heavy pan. Bring to a boil. Let cool.

Using an electric mixer, beat butter and sugar until fluffy. Beat in eggs one at a time. Mix in vanilla and ½ of flour mixture, then add date mixture. Blend in rest of flour. Pour batter into pan. Bake 45 minutes or until top of cake is golden.

Pour ¾ cup of sauce over top, reserving the rest until time to serve, and bake 15 more minutes or until a toothpick inserted in the center comes out clean. Cool in pan 10 minutes and invert onto plate.

MAKE AHEAD: The sauce and cake can be made the day before. Wrap the cake well and store at room temperature: however, store sauce in refrigerator. Best if both cake and sauce are served hot: slowly reheat the sauce. Cut into slices and pour hot sauce over each slice.

Desserts

Ginger Steamed Pudding

1½ C	brown sugar, packed
½ lb	unsalted butter, softened
5	eggs, slightly beaten
2½ C	flour
2 T	ground ginger
1½ t	baking soda
1 C	crystallized ginger, chopped
¾ C	almonds, toasted and chopped
1 T	brandy

Cream sugar and butter together until light. Add slightly beaten eggs to mixture and mix well. Add the combined flour, ground ginger, and baking soda. Mix well. Stir in the crystallized ginger and almonds, and add the brandy. Spoon mixture into buttered mold with a center hole and cover with foil (Almost any bowl that splays out is suitable. Cooking time will be longer if there is no center hole).

Place mold into large pot of boiling water, enough to cover ⅔ up the sides of the mold. Reduce heat, cover and simmer 1½ hours or more until firm. Remove from water and let cool about 10 minutes or until you can unmold it. Once unmolded, cool slightly and serve with whipped cream and a garnish of mint.

Desserts

Mocha Cheesecake

1¼ C	chocolate cookie crumbs
¼ C	sugar
¼ C	butter, melted
8 oz	cream cheese, softened
14 oz	sweetened condensed milk
⅔ C	chocolate syrup
2 t	instant coffee in 1 T of hot water or
	1 T very strong brewed coffee
1 C	heavy whipping cream

For the crust, combine the cookie crumbs, sugar, and melted butter. Press in a 9-inch spring form pan or 10-inch shallow casserole.

Prepare the coffee (strain if coffee doesn't all dissolve) and cool. Whip the heavy cream until stiff peaks form, set aside.

Whip the cream cheese until smooth. Mix in the milk, syrup, and coffee. Fold in the whipped cream until well-blended. Pour into crust and freeze at least 6 hours. Serve frozen and garnish with semi-sweet chocolate shavings.

Desserts

Key Lime Cheesecake

1½ C	graham cracker crumbs
6 T	butter, melted
24 oz	cream cheese, softened
1 C	white sugar
1 T	lime zest, grated
1 T	cornstarch
3	eggs
⅔ C	bottled key lime juice

Preheat oven to 300°. Combine graham cracker crumbs with butter. Press into bottom and partially up sides of 9-inch spring form pan. Refrigerate.

In a large bowl, beat with an electric mixer the cream cheese, sugar, lime peel, and cornstarch until smooth and fluffy. Beat in eggs one at a time, blending just until smooth. Add key lime juice with mixer on low. Finish mixing by hand. Do not over beat or cheesecake will crack during baking. Pour batter into prepared crust. Bake at 300° for 55-60 minutes or until set. To minimize cracking, place a shallow pan half full of water on lower rack during baking.

Turn oven off and let cheesecake stand in oven for 30 minutes with door open at least 4 inches. Refrigerate cheesecake overnight before serving.

Desserts

Raspberry Cream Cheese Coffee Cake

2¼ C	flour
¾ C	sugar
¾ C	butter
½ t	baking powder
½ t	baking soda
¼ t	salt
¾ C	sour cream
1	egg
1 t	almond extract
8 oz	cream cheese, softened
¼ C	sugar
1	egg
½ C	raspberry preserves
½ C	sliced almonds

Preheat oven to 350°. Grease and flour bottom and sides of 9 or 10-inch spring form pan. In large bowl, combine flour and ¾ cup sugar. Using pastry blender or fork, cut in butter until mixture resembles coarse crumbs. Reserve 1 cup crumb mixture. To remaining crumb mixture, add baking powder, baking soda, salt, sour cream, 1 egg, and almond extract; blend well. Spread batter over bottom and 2 inches up sides of prepared pan. (Batter should be about ¼-inch thick on sides.)

In small bowl, combine cream cheese, ¼ cup sugar and 1 egg; blend well. Pour over batter in pan. Carefully spoon preserves evenly over cheese filling. In small bowl, combine 1 cup reserved crumb mixture and sliced almonds. Sprinkle over top.

Bake for 45-55 minutes or until cream cheese filling is set and crust is deep golden brown. Cool 15 minutes. Remove sides of pan. Serve warm or cool; cut into wedges. Refrigerate leftovers.

Desserts

Lemon Tease

3 oz	lemon gelatin
1 C	boiling water
3 T	fresh lemon juice
16 oz	heavy cream, well chilled
8 oz	cream cheese, softened
1 C	sugar
½ t	vanilla
24	ladyfingers, soft cake variety
	lemon peel curls or fresh fruit for garnish

Dissolve gelatin in boiling water and cool to room temperature. Stir in lemon juice. Whip cream until stiff peaks form, set aside.

Cream together cream cheese, sugar, and vanilla. Beat in gelatin mixture. Fold whipped cream into cream cheese and gelatin mixture.

Line sides and bottom of 8-inch buttered spring form pan with ladyfingers. Pour in filling, cover, and chill overnight in refrigerator. To serve place on a serving dish and unmold. Garnish.

Desserts

Berries and Cream Shortcake

1 C	sugar
½ C	butter, softened
2	large eggs
1½ C	cake flour (not self-rising)
1½ t	baking powder
¼ t	salt
½ C	milk
1 t	vanilla extract
1 pt	blueberries
½ pt	strawberries, each cut in half
½ pt	raspberries
½ pt	blackberries
½ C	strawberry or raspberry jam
1 C	heavy cream, well chilled
1 T	sugar

Preheat oven to 350°. Grease and flour two 8 or 9-inch round cake pans. In large bowl, with mixer at low speed, beat 1 cup of sugar with butter just until blended. Increase speed to high; beat until light and fluffy, about 5 minutes. Reduce speed to low; add eggs, then flour, baking powder, salt, vanilla, and milk. Beat until well mixed, constantly scraping bowl with rubber spatula. Increase speed to high; beat 2 minutes, occasionally scraping bowl. Spoon batter into pans.

Bake 25-30 minutes (20-25 for 9-inch), until toothpick inserted in centers of cakes comes out clean. Cool cake layers in pans on wire racks for 10 minutes; remove from pans; cool completely on racks.

Meanwhile, in a large bowl, toss all the berries with the jam. In a medium bowl, with mixer at high speed, beat the cream until soft peaks form. Then add 1 tablespoon of sugar and whip until stiff peaks form.

Place one cake layer on cake plate; spread with half the whipped cream and top with half the fruit mixture. Place second cake layer on fruit mixture; top with remaining whipped cream and fruit. Serve immediately. Refrigerate leftovers.

INSIGHT: All-purpose flour can be substituted for cake flour. Sift the flour two times and gently spoon into a dry measuring cup and level with a straight edged utensil.

Berry Tiramisu

32	ladyfingers, soft cake variety
5	eggs, separated and room temperature
11 T	sugar, divided
2	(8 oz) containers mascarpone cheese, softened
6 T	dark rum, divided
2 t	vanilla, divided
5 C	strawberries (1^1/$_2$ lb) , sliced or raspberries
	berries for garnish

To prepare custard filling, begin by beating the egg whites until foamy. Gradually beat in 2 tablespoons sugar until soft peaks form. Set aside. Whisk the egg yolks and 3 tablespoons sugar over hot water until warm to touch (this dissolves the sugar). Remove and beat on high with an electric mixer until thick and fluffy, about 3 minutes; set aside. Beat mascarpone so it is creamy and then fold mascarpone into the yolk mixture. When blended fold in 2 tablespoons rum and 1 teaspoon vanilla. Next fold in egg whites. Set aside in refrigerator.

For the berry filling combine 4 cups of berries (saving the 5th cup for the sauce), 4 tablespoons rum, and 2 tablespoons sugar. Let stand in refrigerator for 10 minutes.

To assemble, use a 9-inch spring form pan, cover the bottom with ladyfingers filling in all the spaces with broken ladyfingers, it will take about 15. Top with half of the berry filling and then half of the custard filling. Split in half 15 ladyfingers. Place a layer of split ladyfingers and cover with remaining berry filling and custard. Top with remaining split ladyfingers. Wrap the pan in aluminum foil and weight down top with a plate. Refrigerate overnight.

To prepare berry sauce purée 1 cup berries, ^{1}/$_4$ cup sugar, and 1 teaspoon vanilla in a blender or processor. Strain out seeds and refrigerate until ready to serve.

To serve remove sides of spring form pan and sprinkle top of cake with confectioner's sugar. Decorate with whole berries. Drizzle sauce as desired over each slice when served.

Desserts

307

Super-Easy Lemon Tarts

1	lemon about 3" x 3"
1	stick butter, softened
2	eggs
1 C	sugar
6-8	(3") tart shells, 1" deep or 12 (3") shells ½" deep

Preheat oven to 350°. Cut lemon in eighths, removing seeds. Chop lemon, including rind coarsely in food processor. Add sugar, butter (cut into chunks), and eggs. Blend until well-mixed. Pour into 6-8 tart shells and bake 30-35 minutes. Smaller shells take only 20 minutes. Serve warm or cold. Dust with powdered sugar as a garnish.

Desserts

Strawberry-Lemon Tartlets

Almond Crust

1¼ C	flour
½ C	almonds (2 oz), slivered and blanched
¼ C	sugar
¼ t	salt
½ C	chilled unsalted butter, cut into pieces
¾ t	almond extract
2 T	ice water

Filling

¼ C	purchased lemon curd
2 t	lemon peel, grated
¼ C	whipping cream, chilled
16	large strawberries

Glaze

2 T	apricot preserves
2 t	brandy
	lemon peel strips (optional)

Crust: Blend flour, almonds, sugar, and salt in processor until nuts are finely ground. Add butter and cut in using on/off turns until mixture resembles coarse meal. Mix in almond extract and enough water to form moist clumps. Knead dough briefly on work surface to combine; flatten into disk. Wrap in plastic; refrigerate until firm before rolling, at least 2 hours and up to 1 day.

Tartlets: Preheat oven to 375°. Roll out dough on lightly floured surface to 16-inch round (scant ⅛-inch thick). Cut out 3½-inch rounds. Reroll dough scraps to make 16 rounds. Line 3-inch diameter fluted tartlet pans or muffin tins with ½-inch-high sides with dough rounds. Freeze crusts for 15 minutes. Arrange tartlet pans on a large baking sheet. Bake crusts until pale golden, piercing bottoms with toothpick if crusts bubble, about 13 minutes. Cool crusts completely. Turn crusts out of pans.

Filling: Whisk lemon curd and lemon peel in medium bowl until smooth. Whip cream in another medium bowl until soft peaks form. Fold cream into lemon curd in 2 additions. Divide filling among crusts. Cut each strawberry as desired and place 1 atop each tartlet.

Glaze: Stir preserves and brandy in small saucepan over medium heat until mixture comes to boil. Strain into small bowl. Brush each berry with glaze. Garnish tartlets with lemon peel, if desired. Can be prepared 6 hours ahead. Cover loosely and refrigerate.

Desserts

309

Lemon Custard

2 T	butter, softened
1½ C	sugar
4	eggs, separated
4 T	flour
2 C	milk
⅓ C	lemon juice (2 lemons)
2 t	lemon rind, grated

Preheat oven to 325°. Beat butter and sugar with mixer until well blended. Add egg yolks one at a time until smooth. Alternate flour and milk, beating until blended. Add lemon juice and rind and stir. Beat egg whites until stiff but not dry. Fold in sugar mixture, gently yet thoroughly.

Grease with butter 8 (6 oz) custard cups. Spoon custard mix into cups and place them in large baking pan. Fill pan 1-inch deep with water and bake 45 minutes. May serve warm or cold. Garnish with fruit slices, raspberry sauce, or a dusting of confectioners sugar.

Desserts

Lemon Layer Cream Cheese Pie

1   9" refrigerated pie crust

Filling
⅔ C   sugar
2 T   cornstarch
1 C   cold water
2   egg yolks
3 T   lemon juice
1 T   butter
2 t   lemon peel, grated
⅓ C   sugar
8 oz   cream cheese, softened
1   egg

Topping
½ C   heavy cream, whipped

Preheat oven to 375°. Prepare pie crust and refrigerate until filling is ready.

In medium saucepan, combine ⅔ cup sugar and cornstarch; mix well. Gradually add cold water, stirring constantly until blended. In small bowl, beat egg yolks slightly; stir into sugar mixture in saucepan. Cook over medium heat for 10 minutes or until mixture comes to a boil, stirring constantly. Boil one minute. Remove from heat. Stir in lemon juice, butter, and lemon peel; blend well.

In a small bowl, combine ⅓ cup sugar and cream cheese; beat until smooth. Add egg; blend well. Spoon and gently spread cream cheese mixture in prepared crust. Spoon lemon mixture over cream cheese mixture; spread carefully to cover.

Bake for 35-40 minutes or until crust is golden brown. (Center will not be set.) Cool 30 minutes. Refrigerate 1½ hours or until completely chilled; continue to store in the refrigerator. Serve topped with whipped cream.

Desserts

311

Savannah Pecan Pie

3	eggs
⅔ C	sugar
⅛ t	salt
1 C	light corn syrup
6 T	butter, melted
2 C	pecan pieces
1	unbaked 9" pie shell (for deep pie) or 2 (8") for regular pie

Preheat oven to 350°. Beat eggs; beat in sugar, salt, corn syrup, and butter. Add pecan pieces; pour into unbaked pie shell(s). Bake for 50 minutes (for deep pie) or until knife inserted half way between center and edge comes out clean. Cool. For variation, add 1 cup chocolate chips.

Desserts

Ken's Favorite Peanut Butter Pie

1	9" graham cracker crust
8 oz	cream cheese, softened
8 oz	whipped topping, thawed
1 C	creamy peanut butter
¾ C	sugar
1 T	vanilla
	whipped topping, thawed for garnish

Cream all ingredients together in mixing bowl. Pour into crust, cover and freeze until firm, 3-4 hours or overnight. Remove from freezer and thaw. To serve, top with additional whipped topping.

INSPIRATION: This is also good with chocolate sauce drizzled over the top or use a chocolate cookie crust.

Desserts

Strawberry Pie

8 oz	cream cheese, softened
½ t	almond extract
½ C	sugar
1 C	heavy cream, whipped
	oreo cookie crust (or any other kind of crust)
	fresh strawberries, washed, hulled, and dried
	chocolate chips

Beat cream cheese with almond extract and sugar. Fold in whipped cream. Pour into crust. Top with whole berries pointed end up. Melt some chocolate chips and drizzle over top. Refrigerate several hours.

INSIGHT: To whip heavy cream, have cream, bowl, and beaters chilled before whipping on high speed. If additional ingredients and flavorings are to be added, whip only to form soft peaks then add ingredients and continue to whip until firm peaks form. Whipped cream used for a dessert topping should be medium-stiff peaks. Over whipping will turn cream into butter. Store whipped cream, covered, in refrigerator. It will hold for 2-3 hours.

Desserts

Cathy's Best Strawberry Pie

4-5 C	medium, whole strawberries, hulled
1 C	strawberries, crushed
1 C	water
¾ C	sugar
3 T	cornstarch
1	(8 oz) container whipped topping, thawed
1	9" pie crust, baked and cooled

Bring crushed strawberries and one cup of water to a boil. Simmer for 5 minutes. Strain and reserve juice. Into the strained juice add sugar and cornstarch. Cook over medium heat until thick and clear. Cool to room temperature.

Put a thin layer of whipped topping on the bottom of the baked pie shell. Add a thin layer of berry glaze. Place whole berries on top and cover with remaining glaze.

Refrigerate for a few hours. When serving add whipped topping to the top of each slice.

Desserts

White Chocolate Crème Brulée

4	large eggs, at room temperature and separated
⅓ C	sugar
2 C	heavy cream
1	(4 oz) bar high quality white chocolate, chopped into small pieces
½ t	vanilla extract

Preheat oven to 300°. In medium bowl, whisk egg yolks with sugar until smooth, set aside.

In 2-quart saucepan, bring cream to a simmer over medium-high heat. Add white chocolate and turn off heat; whisk until white chocolate is melted. Add white chocolate mixture to egg yolk mixture one tablespoon at a time, whisking continuously to prevent eggs from scrambling. Whisk until smooth. Add vanilla. Pour into four ramekins or custard cups.

Place cups in 13 x 9-inch baking pan or broiler pan. Add enough water so cups sit in 1-1½-inch of water. Bake until set, about 45 minutes. Serve warm, at room temperature, or refrigerate overnight.

INSPIRATION: For a delicious crunchy surface, sprinkle the tops of the crème brulée with 1 teaspoon of sugar and place under broiler until caramelized.

Desserts

Chocolate Mousse

¼ C	sugar
⅓ C	water
2 C	heavy cream, well chilled
8 oz	semi-sweet chocolate chips
3 T	Triple Sec
3	egg yolks

Combine sugar and water in a small pan and boil 3 minutes. Set aside. In a food processor with metal blade, process the cream uninterrupted until firm peaks form, only about 50-60 seconds. Transfer to a large bowl. Reinsert blade and add chocolate. Process turning on and off for 15-20 seconds. Continue processing and gradually add hot syrup, Triple Sec, and yolks until just combined. Pour over whipped cream and fold together.

Finished mousse can be poured into individual cups, ramekins, or into a 7-inch bowl. Immediately cover and refrigerate. Remove just before serving. Any leftovers should be refrigerated right away because of uncooked eggs.

Desserts

317

Mamma Luciana's Fruit Jam Crostata

2½ C	flour
½ t	salt
¾ C	sugar
1 t	cinnamon
4½ oz	almonds or hazelnuts, ground
1	lemon, zest grated
2	eggs, plus 1 egg yolk
8½ T	butter, cut into pieces and slightly softened
2 C	finest quality fruit preserves, any flavor

Preheat oven to 375°. Sift flour into a medium bowl. Stir in all remaining ingredients except eggs, butter, and jam. Make a well in the center in the flour mixture, and add the eggs and butter. Work the mixture with your hands until you are able to form a ball.

Roll dough on a floured surface to the thickness of about ¼-inch. Take a little more than half of the dough and mold it into a 10-inch tart pan with removable bottom. Spread the jam evenly over the dough. Cut the remaining dough into strips, and use them to make a crisscross pattern on top of the jam, and make a border around the edge of the crostata. Bake at 375° for about 30 minutes, or until the dough is just golden. Serve warm.

Desserts

Rocky Mountain High Apple Crisp

5 C	tart apples, peeled and sliced
1 t	cinnamon
1 t	lemon peel, grated
1 t	orange peel, grated
2 T	orange liqueur
2 T	almond liqueur
¾ C	sugar
¾ C	flour
6 T	butter
¼ C	brown sugar, firmly packed
¼ t	salt
	whipped cream or ice cream

Preheat oven to 350°. Grease 2-quart round baking dish. Arrange apple slices in bottom of dish. Sprinkle evenly with cinnamon, lemon peel, orange peel, orange and almond liqueurs. Combine sugar, flour, butter, brown sugar, and salt in medium bowl and mix until crumbly. Sprinkle over apples. Bake until golden brown, about 1 hour. Spoon into bowls. Serve with whipped cream or ice cream.

Desserts

Peach and Blueberry Crisp

1½ lbs	peaches (about 3), pitted and cut into ½" thick wedges
1½ C	blueberries or blackberries
1 T	cornstarch
2 T	fresh lemon juice
⅓ C	sugar
⅔ C	flour
¾ C	light brown sugar, firmly packed
½ C	old-fashioned rolled oats
½ t	salt
1 t	cinnamon
½ t	freshly grated nutmeg
6 T	cold unsalted butter, cut into bits
¾ C	lightly toasted pecans, coarsely chopped (optional)

Preheat the oven to 375°. In a large bowl toss the peaches and the blueberries gently with the cornstarch, the lemon juice, and the granulated sugar until the mixture is combined well. In a small bowl stir together the flour, brown sugar, oats, salt, cinnamon, and nutmeg. Add the butter, blending the mixture until it resembles coarse meal, and stir in the pecans. Spread the peach mixture in a 9x13-inch or 3-quart baking dish, and sprinkle the pecan mixture evenly over it, and bake the crisp for 45-50 minutes, or until the top is golden.

Desserts

Peaches and Brandy

2	fresh, medium, ripe peaches
½ t	lemon juice
¾ C	water
½ C	sugar
2 oz	brandy (or cognac)
	vanilla ice cream

Wash, peel, and quarter the peaches. Set them aside in water with a ½ teaspoon of lemon juice to preserve the color.

In a medium saucepan, add ¾ cup of water and sugar and bring to a boil. Once the sugar has dissolved completely, add the peaches and cover. Reduce heat to medium for 5-7 minutes, or until peaches begin to soften. Remove cover from saucepan and reduce sugar solution by half.

Remove pan from burner and add brandy (or cognac), return pan to burner and flame brandy to burn off alcohol. Scoop ice cream into bowls and immediately spoon hot peach mixture over ice cream.

Desserts

Yogurt Lemon Ice

1¼ C	plain yogurt
3 T	heavy cream
¾ C	sugar
1 C	lemon juice

Mix yogurt, cream, and sugar until sugar is dissolved. Stir in lemon juice. To freeze follow instructions for you ice cream maker.

Desserts

Lime or Lemon Sorbet

2	limes or lemons
2 C	water
1½ C	sugar
⅔ C	fresh lime or lemon juice

Using a vegetable peeler, cut peel (colored part only) from the fruit. Combine
1 cup of water, sugar, and peel in medium sauce pan. Stir over medium heat
until sugar dissolves. Increase heat; bring to a boil. Remove from heat.
Discard peel. Cool syrup and then mix with juice and remaining 1 cup of water.
Chill until cold. To freeze, follow instructions for your ice cream maker.

*INSPIRATION: For a light refreshing dessert, serve the sorbet with our Mexican
Chocolate Cookies (see Index).*

Desserts

Peach Ice

2 C	fresh peaches, peeled and chopped (or frozen, thawed)
½ C	sugar
1 T	fresh lemon juice
2 T	fresh orange juice
⅛ t	cardamom seeds, crushed
2 C	cold water
⅓ C	light corn syrup

In a sauce pan, combine peaches, sugar, lemon juice, orange juice, and cardamom seeds. Cook over medium heat, uncovered for 10 minutes. Stir occasionally. Let cool. In a blender or food processor, mix cooked peach mixture, water, and corn syrup. To freeze follow instructions for your ice cream maker.

Desserts

Frosted Grapes

1	egg white
½ t	water
2-3 T	granulated sugar or as needed
1 lb	seedless green grapes, washed and dried

Beat egg white slightly with ½ teaspoon water in a small bowl. Place 2-3 tablespoons of granulated sugar in a small dish. Dip small bunches of grapes into egg-white mixture, and then into the sugar turning to coat grapes well, sprinkling with more sugar as needed. Place on a rack and dry at room temperature for about 3 hours.

INSPIRATION: Use the frosted grapes to decorate a cheese tray or desserts on a holiday buffet.

Desserts

Strawberries in Balsamic Vinegar

40	strawberries, cut in quarters
3 T	sugar
4 t	balsamic vinegar (good quality)

Purée 10 whole strawberries to use as a base for the sauce. Add the sugar and balsamic vinegar and mix until the sugar is dissolved. Pour the sauce over the cut strawberries and refrigerate for at least 30 minutes prior to serving.

INSPIRATION: This makes a refreshing fat free dessert.

Desserts

Chocolate Dipped Strawberries

1 lb	bittersweet or dark chocolate
1 T	vegetable shortening
1 pt	strawberries, washed and well-dried

Melt chocolate and vegetable shortening over very low heat, slowly. Remove from heat and stir to cool slightly for about a minute. Dip strawberries halfway into the chocolate. Lay each berry on its side on waxed paper. When all are done place in refrigerator to set. Chill in refrigerator up to 24 hours.

INSPIRATION: Double-Dipped Strawberries – Prepare an additional recipe using white chocolate. First dip strawberries in melted white chocolate and allow to set completely in a cool room, then dip into dark or bittersweet chocolate recipe allowing a nice line of the white chocolate to remain exposed. You can also dip the strawberries in toasted crushed almonds after the chocolate.

Desserts

327

Oatmeal Lace Cookies

1 C	butterscotch morsels (6 oz)
¾ C	butter
2 T	boiling water
1 t	baking soda
2 C	rolled oats
1 C	sifted flour
¾ C	sugar
dash	salt

Preheat oven to 350°. Combine morsels and butter and melt in a double boiler or in microwave. Remove from heat. Mix boiling water with baking soda. Add to butterscotch mixture. Gradually blend in remaining ingredients.

Drop by slightly rounded teaspoonfuls onto ungreased baking sheets. Bake 10 minutes.

Makes about 3 dozen cookies.

Oatmeal Cranberry White Chocolate Cookies

1 C	butter, softened
1 C	light brown sugar
2	eggs
2 C	oats
2 C	flour
½ t	salt
1 t	baking soda
1½ C	dried cranberries
1 C	white chocolate chunks or chips

Preheat oven to 375°. Beat butter and brown sugar until light and creamy. Add eggs, one at a time, beating well after each addition. Combine oats, flour, salt and baking soda in a separate mixing bowl. Add wet mixture to dry mixture in several stages, mixing well after each addition. Stir in dried cranberries and chocolate chips, mixing just to combine.

Drop by rounded teaspoonfuls onto an ungreased cookie sheet. Bake 10-12 minutes or until golden brown.

Makes about 5 dozen.

Oatmeal Cookies

¾ C	butter, softened
1 C	brown sugar
½ C	sugar
1	egg
¼ C	water
¼-½ t	cinnamon
1 t	vanilla
1 C	flour
1 t	salt
½ t	baking soda
3 C	oats
1 C	nuts, chopped, optional
1 C	raisins, optional

Preheat oven to 350°. Place butter, sugar, egg, water, cinnamon and vanilla in bowl. Beat thoroughly. Sift together flour, salt, and soda. Blend in oats, raisins, and nuts. Drop by teaspoons onto greased cookie sheets. Bake for 12-15 minutes.

Makes about 5 dozen.

INSPIRATION: If using raisins, try soaking them in ⅓ cup dark rum; simmer raisins and rum for 10-12 minutes, then let steep for 20 minutes before adding to cookie batter. Drain raisins well before adding.

Anzac Crispies

1 C	rolled oats
1 C	flour
¾ C	coconut
1 C	sugar
½ C	butter
1 T	golden syrup or honey
1½ t	baking soda
2 T	boiling water

Preheat oven to 300°. Mix oats, flour, sugar, and coconut together. Melt syrup and butter together. Mix soda with boiling water and add to melted ingredients (butter and syrup). Add to dry ingredients.

Place tablespoons of dough onto a greased or parchment lined cookie sheet. Bake for 20 minutes.

Makes 3 dozen.

INSIGHT: This is an Australian recipe dating from the First World War. Anzac stands for Australia and New Zealand Air Corps. The Australian women sent these biscuits to the soldiers fighting over seas.

Desserts

Amaretti-Mascarpone Cookies

2	(7 oz) pkg amaretti cookies
8 oz	mascarpone cheese
¼ C	freshly brewed espresso
1	(7 oz) bag coconut flakes, finely chopped
1 C	powdered sugar, divided

Combine mascarpone cheese with ⅓-½ cup powdered sugar, depending on desired sweetness. In separate bowl, combine ¼-½ cup powdered sugar with the coconut flakes.

Take two amaretti cookies and spread cheese mixture on the flat side of the cookies and form a sandwich. Brush or dunk with espresso. Do not soak too heavily or the amaretti mascarpone cookie will become too soggy. Then roll the cookie in coconut/sugar mixture. Repeat the process using the remaining cookies. Store the cookies between layers of wax paper in the refrigerator.

When serving the cookies, experiment with different designs when placing the cookies on the platter (making a pyramid pattern, a star pattern, etc.) Sprinkle any remaining coconut/sugar mixture on top of cookies.

Desserts

Mexican Chocolate Cookies

1 C	flour
½ C+1 T	unsweetened Dutch process cocoa powder
½ t	cinnamon
¼ t	baking soda
¼ t	salt
⅛ t	cayenne pepper
⅛ t	freshly ground black or white pepper
½ C+1 T	light brown sugar, lightly packed
½ C+1 T	sugar
6 T	unsalted butter, at room temperature
1 t	vanilla extract
1	large egg white

In a medium bowl, whisk the flour with the cocoa, cinnamon, baking soda, salt, cayenne, and black pepper. In a small bowl, combine the sugars, pressing out any lumps. In a medium bowl, using an electric mixer, cream butter with the sugars at medium speed until fluffy. Add the vanilla and beat for 1 minute. Beat in the egg white. Reduce the speed to low and beat in the dry ingredients. Gather the dough together and knead it slightly, then form it into a 10-inch log about 2-inches in diameter. Wrap in wax paper and refrigerate until firm, at least 45 minutes.

MAKE AHEAD: The log may be refrigerated for up to 3 days rewrapped in plastic or rewrapped in foil and freeze up to 3 months.

Preheat oven to 350°. Line 2 large cookie sheets with parchment paper or foil. Cut the log of dough crosswise slightly less than ¼-inch thick. Place the cookies about 1-inch apart on the prepared cookie sheets. Bake on the upper and lower racks of the oven for 10-12 minutes, switching the sheets after 5 minutes, until the cookies are crackled and puffed. Transfer the cookies to racks to cool. The cookies will keep for up to 2 weeks in an airtight container or in the freezer for several months. When serving, dust the tops of the cookies with powdered sugar.

Makes about 40 cookies.

"Hot from the Oven" Lumberjack Cookies

1 C	sugar
1 C	shortening
1 C	dark molasses
2	eggs
4 C	flour
1 t	soda
1 t	salt
2 t	cinnamon
1 t	ginger

Cream together the sugar and shortening. Add molasses and unbeaten eggs. Mix well. Sift together dry ingredients and stir in. At this point if dough is too soft to work with, chill in the refrigerator for several hours.

Put ¼ cup sugar in a small bowl. Dip fingers into sugar, then pinch off a ball of dough and roll it to the size and shape of a walnut. Dip the rolled ball into the bowl of sugar. Place balls on greased cookie sheet about 2 inches apart. Bake at 350° for 12-15 minutes.

Makes 4 dozen large, soft cookies.

MAKE AHEAD: This dough keeps up to one week in the refrigerator.

Desserts

Lemon Frosted Nut Bars

Bars

1 C	flour
½ C	butter, softened
2	eggs, beaten
1½ C	dark brown sugar, packed
1½ C	pecans, finely chopped
2 T	flour
½ t	salt
1 t	vanilla

Glaze

1½ C	powdered sugar
2 T	fresh lemon juice (more if needed)

Preheat oven to 350°. Combine 1 cup of flour and the butter until well mixed. Cover bottom of 9 x 13-inch pan. Bake for 12 minutes.

Beat together eggs, dark brown sugar, 2 tablespoons flour, salt, and vanilla. Stir in pecans. Pour over top of butter flour mixture and return to oven for 25 minutes.

To prepare glaze: mix powdered sugar and lemon juice to make a thin frosting and pour sparingly over pan while nut bars are still warm. Once cooled, cut bars and store in an airtight container.

Makes 30-40 bars.

INSIGHT: This recipe dates back to the 1950's and was a favorite in Mississippi Delta where pecans (and parties) were plentiful!

Decadent Brownies

6 oz	semisweet chocolate (chips work well)
¼ C	chocolate syrup
8 T	unsalted butter, room temperature
1 t	vanilla
2	eggs, lightly beaten
¾ C	sugar
	pinch of salt
½ C	flour

Butter and flour an 8-inch square pan. Line bottom and 2 sides with parchment paper for easy lift out of pan. Melt chocolate in small heavy saucepan over low heat, stirring constantly. Add chocolate syrup and stir well. Remove pan from heat and add butter; mix until smooth. Stir in vanilla and eggs; mix well (if using the fresh mint, add this now). In a separate bowl combine flour, sugar, and salt. Add this to chocolate mixture and blend thoroughly. Pour into pan and bake at 350° for 30 minutes. Cool thoroughly.

INSPIRATION: The addition of 1½ tablespoons of chopped fresh mint is delicious. Because this is a gooey melt in your mouth brownie, freeze before cutting and thaw briefly before serving.

Desserts

POST

desserts

everything else

Tomato, Cucumber, and Caper Relish

1	medium English cucumber, unpeeled and diced
12 oz	cherry tomatoes, quartered
1	yellow bell pepper, diced
¼ C	capers, drained and rinsed
2 T	fresh cilantro, chopped

Dressing

2 T	olive oil
2 T	fresh lemon juice
2 T	shallots, chopped
2 t	lemon peel, grated
1 t	cumin

Mix together dressing. Toss with vegetables, capers, and cilantro. Season with salt and pepper. Let stand 30 minutes, stirring occasionally. Serve with grilled or roasted fish, especially salmon.

Makes about 3 cups.

Roasted Red Bell Pepper Relish with Garlic, Capers, and Parsley

3	large red bell peppers
3 T	fresh Italian parsley, chopped
3 T	capers, drained
2 T	extra-virgin olive oil
1-2	cloves garlic, minced
2 t	balsamic vinegar

Char bell peppers over gas flame or in broiler until blackened on all sides. Enclose in bag, let stand for 10 minutes. Peel, seed, and finely chop peppers. Transfer to medium bowl. Add remaining ingredients. Season to taste with salt and pepper. This can be prepared 6 hours ahead and refrigerated. Serve with grilled salmon or shrimp.

Makes about 1½ cups.

INSPIRATION: Serve this as an appetizer spread on French rounds.

Artichoke Relish

1	(14 oz) can artichoke hearts, drained and chopped
3	roma tomatoes, seeded and diced
½	red onion, diced
6-8	pitted kalamata olives, diced
1 T	capers, drained and rinsed
½ t	salt
½ t	black pepper
2 T	fresh basil, chopped
¼ C	olive oil
3 T	balsamic vinegar
	feta cheese, garnish

Mix relish ingredients together and let stand for 2-6 hours. Serve with grilled fish and garnish with feta cheese to taste.

Tri-flavored Relish

½ C	bell pepper, diced
½ C	sweet onion, diced
¼ C	green onions, minced
2 T	fresh Italian parsley, minced
2 T	extra-virgin olive oil
1 T	fresh lemon juice
1 T	fresh orange juice
1 T	orange pulp, chopped
1 t	orange peel, finely shredded
1 t	fresh oregano leaves, chopped, or ¼ t dried
1 t	fresh thyme leaves, or ⅛ t dried
½ t	salt
⅛ t	freshly ground pepper

Mix all ingredients in large bowl. Can be prepared 4 hours ahead; chill. Serve with grilled fish, especially snapper. Serve cold or at room temperature.

Makes about 1½ cups.

Confetti Pepper Relish

2	sweet red peppers, seeded and chopped
2	green pepper, seeded and chopped
1	large white onion, chopped
1	jalapeño pepper, chopped
½ C	white vinegar
¼ t	salt
½ C	sugar

Combine red and green pepper, onion, and jalapeño pepper in a Dutch oven; add boiling water to cover pepper mixture. Let stand 5 minutes, drain. Combine vinegar, sugar, and salt, stirring well; pour over pepper mixture. Bring to a boil over medium heat; boil 5 minutes, stirring occasionally. Chill. Serve with fish, chicken, ham, or other meats.

Makes 4 cups.

Peach, Onion, and Bell Pepper Salsa

2	firm but ripe unpeeled peaches, cut into ¼" dice
¼ C	green or sweet onions, thinly sliced
2 T	red bell pepper, minced
2 T	green bell pepper, minced
1 T	fresh lime juice
1 T	fresh cilantro, chopped
1 T	fresh Italian parsley, chopped
1 t	olive oil
½ t	ground cumin
¼ t	salt
⅛ t	coarsely ground pepper
1 t	jalapeño chilies, minced or more to taste

Mix all ingredients in a large bowl. Cover and refrigerate for 30 minutes. Add more chilies if a spicier salsa is desired. (Can be prepared 2 hours ahead and refrigerated.) Serve with fish, poultry, or pork.

Makes about 1½ cups.

Fresh Plum Salsa

¼ t	ground cumin
1 T	lime juice
4	medium red or black plums, pitted and cut into medium dice
1	small onion, minced
1 T	cilantro, minced
2	medium hot chiles, such as serrano or jalapeños, minced
1	medium orange, peeled, sectioned, and cut into large dice

Mix all ingredients in a medium nonreactive bowl. Serve with grilled pork or chicken.

Apple Chutney

1	lemon, seeded and chopped
1	garlic clove, chopped
5 C	apples, peeled and chopped
1 lb	brown sugar
1 lb	seedless raisins
¾ C	crystallized ginger, chopped
1½ t	salt
⅛-¼ t	cayenne
2 C	red wine vinegar

Mix ingredients and simmer until tender. Cover and refrigerate. Drain before serving. Delicious served with curried chicken and other meats.

INSPIRATION: To serve as an appetizer, mix 1 or 2 tablespoons with 8 oz cream cheese or spoon over Brie.

Cranberry Relish

1	large orange
½	lemon
1 T	water
1	apple
1 lb	fresh cranberries
1½ C	sugar
1 C	walnuts or pecans, chopped

Cut rind from orange and lemon; try to leave as much of the white as possible on the fruit. Chop rind until fine. Remove white from orange and lemon, and cut fruit into very small pieces. Mix in rind. Place ½ this mixture in food processor with water and cranberries, processing until still slightly chunky. Place in bowl with remaining citrus fruit. Core apple and cut into small chunks. Add to cranberries, along with sugar and nuts.

Store relish in the refrigerator for several days so flavors develop before serving. The relish will keep refrigerated up to 1 month.

Cranberry Ketchup

1	(12 oz) bag whole cranberries, (4½ cups) picked over
2	large onions (3 cups), finely chopped
1⅓ C	white wine vinegar
3	medium garlic cloves, minced
1 T+1t	ground allspice
1 t	salt
¾ C	sugar

In a medium nonreactive saucepan, combine ⅔ cup water with the cranberries, onions, vinegar, garlic, allspice, and salt. Bring to a simmer over moderately low heat and cook, stirring occasionally, until thick and pulpy, about 20 minutes. Stir in the sugar, return to a simmer and cook, stirring frequently, for 15 minutes longer. Let cool for 30 minutes.

Transfer the mixture to a blender and purée, then strain. Pour the ketchup into glass bottles. The ketchup will keep refrigerated for up to 2 months. This is excellent served on a turkey sandwich, hamburger or use in chicken salad.

Makes 3 cups.

Low Fat Hollandaise Sauce

1 T	butter
¾ C	buttermilk
1 T	cornstarch
½ t	salt
pinch	cayenne pepper
1	egg, lightly beaten
1 T	lemon juice
⅛ t	Dijon mustard

In a heavy medium size pan, melt butter and cook while swirling until golden. Pour into small bowl. In the same pan but off the heat, whip buttermilk, cornstarch, salt, and pepper until smooth. Whisk egg into buttermilk mixture. Over medium-low heat, cook while stirring to a simmer. Cook 15 seconds. Remove from heat. Whisk in lemon juice, butter, Dijon. Serve immediately on asparagus, broccoli, or poached eggs. Any sauce left over can be stored in the refrigerator and slowly reheated.

Makes about 1 cup.

Cheese Crisp

½ C   **Gruyere cheese, grated**
1 T   **Parmesan cheese, grated**

Toss both cheeses together in a small bowl. Preheat an 8-inch non-stick skillet over medium heat. Sprinkle cheese in an even layer in preheated skillet. Cook over medium heat, spooning off the fat, until lightly golden brown, about 6 minutes. Using a spatula, carefully lift the pancake onto a paper towel lined baking sheet and gently blot dry. Makes one 8-inch cheese crisp. Repeat ingredients as needed for more cheese crisps.

INSPIRATION: These are good broken into pieces and used as a topping for green salads or soups. You may also break these into larger pieces to serve with a salad or soup on the side.

Sandwich Crowns

6	red bell peppers or 2 (12-14 oz) jars or cans roasted red bell peppers
½ C	olive oil
¼ C	balsamic vinegar
2	small garlic cloves, minced
2	1½ lb round rye, pumpernickel, or white loaves
	Dijon mustard
12	slices hard salami, sliced thin
¼ lb	spinach leaves, trimmed
12	slices provolone cheese, sliced thin
12	red onion rings, sliced thin
12	slices cooked turkey, sliced thin
	oregano
	freshly ground pepper

Drain peppers or roast and peel fresh ones. (Char pepper over gas flame or in broiler until blackened on all sides. Wrap in paper bag and let stand 10 minutes to steam. Peel and seed peppers. Rinse if necessary; pat dry.) Cut into ¾-inch wide strips. Combine oil, vinegar, and garlic in medium bowl. Add peppers and turn to coat. Marinate at least 1 hour at room temperature. Drain peppers.

MAKE AHEAD: The marinated peppers can be prepared 1 day ahead. Cover tightly and refrigerate.

Using serrated knife, cut top third off loaves and reserve. Remove insides of loaves and tops, leaving ½-inch shells. Spread insides of loaves and tops with thin layer of Dijon. Place ½ of salami and spinach in each loaf. Add ¼ of peppers to each. Top with cheese and onion rings, then remaining peppers. Sprinkle with oregano and pepper. Cover with turkey. Replace loaf tops. Wrap each in plastic and foil. Refrigerate overnight.

Cut each into 6 wedges before serving. Offer additional mustard, mayonnaise, and/or olive oil.

INSPIRATION: These sandwich crowns are best prepared the day before serving and are a great menu item for a tailgate party.

Everything Else

Grandma's Banana Bread

SERVES
10

¼ C	butter, softened
1 C	sugar
2	eggs
2 C	flour
1 t	baking soda
½ t	salt
3-4	ripe bananas, mashed
2 t	milk

Preheat oven to 325°. Cream butter and sugar. Add eggs. Mix flour, baking soda, and salt in a separate bowl. Add bananas to butter, sugar, and egg mix along with milk. Add half of flour mixture to banana mixture, blend. Add remaining flour mixture. Mix thoroughly. Bake in a greased loaf pan for 55-60 minutes.

Date Nut Bread

1 C	dates, pitted and coarsely chopped
1½ t	baking soda
3 T	unsalted butter, softened
¾ C	water, boiling
1½ C	flour
1 C	sugar
½ t	salt
2	large eggs, lightly beaten
1 t	vanilla extract
1 C	pecans, chopped

Preheat oven to 325°. Grease a 8 x 4-inch loaf pan. In a medium bowl, toss the dates with the baking soda. Add the butter. Cover with the boiling water and let stand 20 minutes. In another bowl, combine the flour, sugar, and salt. Add the eggs and vanilla and stir to combine. Stir in the pecans and date mixture, combine thoroughly. Pour into the prepared loaf pan. Bake for 55 minutes or until toothpick inserted in the center comes out clean.

Cool in the pan for 10 minutes and then remove onto a cooling rack to cool completely. To store the bread, wrap well and refrigerate up to 5 days. Serve with cream cheese or other soft mild-flavored cheese.

Everything Else

Blueberry – Lemon Bread

¼ C+2 T	butter, softened
1 C	sugar
2	eggs
1½ C	flour
1 t	baking powder
pinch	salt
½ C	milk
2 t	lemon rind, grated
1 C	fresh blueberries, rinsed and dried
⅓ C	sugar
3 T	lemon juice

Preheat oven to 350°. Cream butter; gradually add 1 cup sugar, beating at medium speed of an electric mixer until well blended. Add eggs, one at a time, beating well after each addition. Combine flour, baking powder, and salt; add to creamed mixture alternating with milk, beginning and ending with flour mixture. Stir in grated lemon rind; then fold in blueberries. Pour batter into a greased 8 x 4 x 3-inch loaf pan. Bake for 55 minutes or until a toothpick inserted in center comes out clean.

Combine ⅓ cup sugar and lemon juice in a small saucepan; heat until sugar dissolves. Puncture top of bread in several places with toothpick; pour lemon juice mixture over warm bread, allowing mixture to soak into bread. Cool bread in the pan for 30 minutes.

Lemon Poppy Seed Scones

2 C	flour
3 t	baking powder
¼ t	salt
¼ C	sugar
1 T	poppy seeds
⅓ C	butter
2 T	lemon juice
¾ C	buttermilk or milk
	sugar for dusting

Preheat oven to 425°. Spray cookie sheet with nonstick spray or parchment paper. Mix all dry ingredients and cut in butter using a pastry blender until the mixture is crumbly. Mix in milk or buttermilk and lemon juice. Stir into flour mixture until dough leaves sides of bowl. Turn dough onto lightly floured surface and knead gently 10 times. Roll or pat into a 9-inch circle. Sprinkle with sugar. Cut into 8 wedges. Place on cookie sheet and bake 12-15 minutes or until golden brown. Serve warm.

Corn and Jalapeño Jam Muffins

1½ C	flour
¾ C	cornmeal, stone-ground, medium grind
1 T	baking powder
½ t	salt
¼ t	cayenne
¾ C	buttermilk
¼ C	unsalted butter, melted
3 T	sugar
2	eggs
1½ C	corn kernels, fresh or frozen and thawed
¾ C	jalapeño jelly or jam, or spicy tomato chutney

Preheat the oven to 375°. Grease the muffin tins. Sift together the flour, cornmeal, baking powder, salt, and cayenne in a bowl, and set it aside. In a larger bowl beat together the buttermilk, butter, and sugar. Mix in the eggs, followed by the corn, blending well after each addition. Add the flour mixture, and stir to combine lightly.

Spoon about half of the batter – it will be a bit stiff – into the muffin tins, filling each cup just ⅓ full. Drop a dollop of jelly, about 1 teaspoon, on top of the batter in each cup. Top with the remaining batter covering the jelly completely for each muffin.

Bake the muffins 22-24 minutes (18 minutes for mini), until they are deep golden. Serve them warm. Make some without the spicy filling to please all of the family.

Makes 12 muffins or 36 mini-sized muffins.

Cheese Biscuits

2 C	self-rising flour
1 t	baking powder
1 t	baking soda
¾ C	buttermilk
½ C	vegetable shortening
2 C	sharp or extra sharp Cheddar cheese, grated

Preheat oven to 400°. Mix flour and dry ingredients. Cut in shortening until coarsely mixed. Add buttermilk alternately with cheese (a little at a time). Mix until just blended, do not over mix. Flour work surface and knead dough several times, adding more flour if too wet. Dough should be soft. Then pat or roll out dough to 1-inch thick. Using a 1½-inch biscuit cutter, cut and place on a cookie sheet. Bake until biscuits are light brown, 8-10 minutes. These biscuits freeze well.

Makes 20 biscuits.

Swiss Spinach Pie

8 oz	pkg Swiss cheese, sliced
2 T	flour
1	(10 oz) pkg frozen spinach, chopped
1 C	milk
3	eggs, beaten
1 t	salt
	pepper
dash	nutmeg or cayenne
	9" pre-made pie shell

Preheat oven to 350°. Cut cheese into strips and toss with 2 tablespoons of flour. Thaw spinach and squeeze well to drain. Beat eggs, milk, salt, pepper, and nutmeg or cayenne. Add drained spinach and cheese. Mix together and pour into unbaked pie shell. Bake for 40-45 minutes, or until knife comes out clean when stuck into center of pie.

Chicken Vegetable Quiche

2	frozen deep dish pie crusts
2-4 C	cooked chicken breast, cubed or shredded
1 C	Chedder cheese, grated
1 C	Swiss cheese, grated
1	(10 oz) pkg frozen boccoli florets or spinach, thawed and well drained
1	small onion, chopped
1	red bell pepper, chopped
1	can evaporated milk (can use half evaporated skim milk and half evaporated milk)
½ C	mayonnaise
5	eggs, lightly beaten
½ t	nutmeg
1 t	Worcestershire sauce
	hot sauce, salt and pepper to taste

Preheat oven to 350˚. Fill the two pie crusts evenly with the chicken, cheese, broccoli, onion and red bell pepper. Combine milk, mayonnaise, eggs and seasonings and pour over the filling. Sprinkle the top with a little flour. Bake for 40 minutes or until knife inserted in pie comes out clean.

Everything Else

Green and Red Frittata

8	eggs
2½ T	warm water
4 oz	fontina cheese, cut into small pieces
2 T	olive oil
1	red bell pepper, cut into ½" dice
3	medium zucchini, cut into 1" dice
	salt and pepper to taste
2½ T	fresh oregano, chopped

In a small bowl, lightly beat eggs with warm water. Stir in cheese. Set aside. In a 10-inch braiser or ovenproof fry pan over medium-high heat, heat olive oil. Add zucchini and bell pepper. Season with salt and pepper. Sauté until lightly browned, about 5 minutes. Stir in the oregano. Reduce heat to medium. Add egg and cheese mixture.

Preheat broiler. Once eggs begin to cook, lift edges with spatula so uncooked eggs flow underneath. Repeat until most of egg mixture is cooked. Place pan 6 inches below the heat source of the broiler. Broil until the top of the frittata is puffed and golden, about 3 minutes. Cut into wedges and serve.

Everything Else

Garden Sangria

1 gal	dry white wine
2 C	brandy
1 C	orange liqueur
4	oranges, sliced
1	bunch fresh mint leaves
1 liter	bottle club soda (or ginger ale), chilled
1 qt	strawberries
2	lemons, thinly sliced
2	limes, thinly sliced

Combine white wine, brandy, orange liqueur, oranges, and fresh mint leaves in a large container. Cover and chill for 8 hours.

Add club soda, strawberries, lemons, and limes just before serving. Serve sangria over ice, if desired.

Makes 1$\frac{1}{2}$ gallons.

Iced Tea Concentrate

12	regular-size tea bags or 4 family-size
4$\frac{1}{2}$ C	water

In a 2-quart saucepan, bring the water to a boil. Remove from heat and add the tea bags which have their strings secured together. Cover and steep 15-20 minutes, stirring gently once or twice to release flavor. Remove the tea bags; do not squeeze them, which can add bitterness. Let cool at room temperature. Pour concentrated tea into glass jars with plastic lids and store in refrigerator up to 1 week.

Makes about 1 quart concentrate.

INSIGHT: Over-steeping the teabags causes bitterness. Allow the tea to cool at room temperature because hot tea put into the refrigerator turns cloudy.

Refreshing Iced Tea

2 C	iced tea concentrate
6 C	cold water

Flavoring choices

½ C	fresh lemon juice
1 t	fruit syrup
	sugar or artificial sweetener to taste
	fruit nectar

Combine tea and water. Add flavoring to taste or serve over ice offering lemon wedges, sugar, and mint on the side.

Makes 2 quarts.

Ambrosia Shake

4	fully ripe bananas
$1/3$ C	orange juice
$1/2$ t	vanilla extract
4 C	skim or low-fat milk

Blend all ingredients at medium speed for one minute or until desired consistency is reached.

Calories: 115 per cup.

COOK'S NOTES

TFM Cookbook Index

COOK'S NOTES

COOK'S NOTES

substitutions

1 oz unsweetened chocolate ....3 T cocoa + 1 T fat

1 c buttermilk ....1 T lemon juice or white vinegar
+ milk to fill 1 c (let stand 5 minutes)

1 c whole milk ....½ c evaporated milk + ½ c water

1 c half & half ....1 ½ T butter + ⅞ c milk or 1 c evaporated milk

1 c heavy cream ....⅓ c butter + ¾ c milk (will not whip)

1 c sour cream..................................1 T lemon juice + evaporated milk to fill 1 c

1 T cornstarch ....2 T all purpose flour

1 t baking powder............................¼ t baking soda + ½ t cream of tartar

1 c cake flour...................................⅞ c all purpose flour, then sift

1 c self-rising flour...........................1 c all purpose flour + 1 t baking power + ½ t salt

1 clove garlic ....⅛ t garlic powder

1 T fresh herbs ....1 t dried herbs

1 t allspice ....½ t cinnamon + ½ t ground cloves

1 T ginger, candied or raw..............⅛ t powdered ginger

1 T lemon grass...............................1 T lemon peel

1 t lemon juice ....½ t vinegar

1 t mustard, dry...............................1 T prepared mustard

1 lb fresh mushrooms.......................12 oz canned mushrooms

roasting temperatures

Temperatures are most accurately determined by using an instant-read thermometer inserted in the thickest part of the meat, not touching any bone. These are in-oven temperatures. As the meat rests for 5 - 10 minutes, the temperature will increase approximately 5°.

beef
125°F ....rare
130°F - 135°F.................medium-rare
135°F - 140°F.................medium
155°F ....well done

lamb
130°F ....rare
135°F ....medium-rare
140°F ....medium
160°F ....well done

pork & veal 150°F ....medium

poultry
chicken breast................160°F
chicken thigh ....165°F
turkey breast..................165°F